ROCKY M   N
NATIONAL PARK
A Wildlife Watcher's Guide

By Todd Wilkinson
Photography by Michael H. Francis

NORTHWORD
PRESS, INC
Minocqua, Wisconsin

Library of Congress Cataloging-in-Publication Data
Wilkinson, Todd.
    Rocky Mountain National Park : a wildlife watcher's guide / by
Todd Wilkinson ; [photography by Michael H. Francis].
        p.   cm. -- (Wildlife watcher's guide)
    Includes bibliographical references.
    ISBN 1-55971-227-9 : $11.95
    1. Wildlife watching--Colorado--Rocky Mountain National Park-
-Guidebooks.   2. Wildlife viewing sites--Colorado--Rocky Mountain
National Park--Guidebooks.   I. Francis, Michael H. (Michael
harlowe), 1953-   .   II. Title.   III. Series : Wildlife watcher's
guide series.
QL165.W55   1994
599.09788'69--dc20   93-45668
                                                                    CIP

© 1994 NorthWord Press, Inc.
P.O. Box 1360, Minocqua, WI 54548

Edited by Greg Linder
Designed by West 44th Street Graphics, Minneapolis, MN

All photography by Michael H. Francis except for
p. 76 by Wendy Shattil / Bob Rozinski and p. 77 by W. Perry Conway

For a free catalog describing NorthWord's
line of nature books and gifts, call 1-800-336-5666

ISBN 1-55971-2279

Printed and bound in Singapore

TABLE OF CONTENTS

ROCKY MOUNTAIN PARK MAP 8
INTRODUCTION 10
WILDLIFE WATCHER'S CODE OF CONDUCT 13
WILDLIFE ENCOUNTERS CHART 16
TIPS FOR FINDING WILDLIFE 18
THE GREAT DIVIDE 21
BEGINNING YOUR ADVENTURE 22

MAMMALS
Bighorn Sheep 25
Elk (Wapiti) 28
Mule Deer 33
Moose 36
Black Bear 38
Mountain Lion 42
Bobcat 44
Coyote 46
Red Fox 49
Badger 50
River Otter 52
Beaver 54
Porcupine 56
Snowshoe Hare 58
Yellow-Bellied Marmot 60
Abert's Squirrel 61
Pika 63

BIRDS
Golden Eagle 65
Bald Eagle 67
Red-Tailed Hawk 68
Peregrine Falcon 70
Clark's Nutcracker 71
Steller's Jay 73
Mountain Bluebird 74
Broad-Tailed Hummingbird 75
Western Tanager 76
White-Tailed Ptarmigan 78
Water Pipit 79

A ROCKY MOUNTAIN GALLERY 81
SO YOU'D LIKE TO KNOW MORE? 92
BIBLIOGRAPHY 94

ABOUT THIS GUIDE

Rocky Mountain National Park: A Wildlife Watcher's Guide is designed to make your search for mammals and birds within Rocky Mountain National Park as simple and informed as possible. From bighorn sheep to broad-tailed hummingbirds, from elk to golden eagles, there is no better companion for leading you to the best wildlife viewing spots.

This guide offers tips to help you find over 50 species of animals that are sometimes observed from the roadside. By using narratives, color photographs, maps, charts, tracks, and specific recommendations concerning where to travel, visitors of all ages can embark upon their own wildlife safaris.

Author Todd Wilkinson and photographer Michael H.Francis have collaborated on several projects designed to assist readers in viewing wildlife throughout the Rockies. If you have suggestions for future editions of this guide, please send them to: Editor, NorthWord Press, Box 1360, Minocqua, WI 54548.

ACKNOWLEDGMENTS

We extend special thanks to Jeff Maugans, Rocky Mountain's Fall River District naturalist, who reviewed the text, was generous with his time, and provided numerous suggestions for improving this guide. Two others worthy of special mention are park spokesman Doug Caldwell and seasonal naturalist Rebecca Ditgen, both of whom were very helpful in providing information and insight.

We applaud all of the dedicated rangers at Rocky Mountain National Park. They have worked tirelessly to assist visitors even though they are forced to provide more services with less funding each year. We offer our appreciation, too, to the Rocky Mountain Nature Association, which helps educate millions of visitors about park wonders each year.

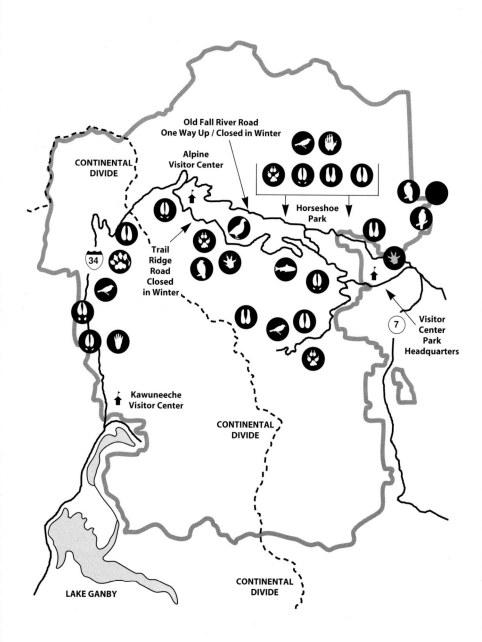

Old Fall River Road
One Way Up / Closed in Winter

Alpine
Visitor Center

CONTINENTAL
DIVIDE

Horseshoe
Park

Trail
Ridge
Road
Closed
in Winter

34

7

Visitor
Center
Park
Headquarters

Kawuneeche
Visitor Center

CONTINENTAL
DIVIDE

CONTINENTAL
DIVIDE

LAKE GANBY

ROCKY MOUNTAIN NATIONAL PARK

 Beavers

 Bighorn Sheep

 Birds

 Coyotes

 Eagles

 Elk

 Falcons

 Hawks

 Marmots

Moose

Mule Deer

Pika

 Ptarmigan

 Raccoons

River Otters

Trout

INTRODUCTION

Rocky Mountain National Park
A Wildlife Paradise in the Colorado Rockies

Before Rocky Mountain National Park was created in 1915, this portion of the Colorado Rockies was already cherished by Native Americans, fur trappers, big-game hunters, and settlers. With more than 60 summits topping 12,000 feet in elevation, the landscape alone could refresh one's spirit. Like the three million people who will visit the park this year, the earliest travelers also recognized the area's value as a rich wildlife reservoir. Over 250 bird and 50 mammal species reside during all or part of the year in this 415-square-mile reserve, which is located just over an hour away from metropolitan Denver.

Recent surveys show that eight of every ten visitors in Rocky Mountain come to the park to view wildlife. While these wildlife safaris are enormously popular, they present challenges for park managers. Rocky Mountain National Park encompasses only one-eighth as much land as Yellowstone, yet each park entertains the same number of visitors. This means that people and wildlife are in close quarters within Rocky Mountain. The only means of ensuring that wildlife populations survive is to minimize human impact upon habitat and other resources. Approaching the landscape with sensitivity is the first step all visitors can take toward becoming responsible wildlife watchers.

Rocky Mountain's high elevation gives it what few other places in the Lower 48 can offer—an abundance of alpine tundra. Above treeline, hardy lichens, mosses, wildflowers, and shrubs have evolved on summits perpetually bombarded by cold and wind. Despite the alpine tundra's rugged appearance, however, it is the most fragile ecosystem in the park, so travelers must take special care to preserve its breathtaking beauty. Merely by stepping off a trail, a hiker can cause damage to fragile plant communities that may take hundreds of years to heal. So special is this ecosystem that Rocky Mountain is part of a worldwide monitoring effort to gauge the potential effects of global warming on indigenous flora and fauna.

Wildlife in the park traverse several ecosystems in addition to alpine tundra. One word that visitors will see frequently on a park map is the word "park" itself, used to describe certain geographical locales within the national park. In Western jargon, such a "park" is an open meadow surrounded by forest. Parks are ideal places for wildlife watching, because many species hunt or forage near the junction of meadows and forests. This book will direct readers to several parks within Rocky Mountain that are premier viewing areas.

"All the wild animals you expect to find in the high country are in Rocky Mountain; but the elk and the mule deer are especially abundant," wrote Freeman Tilden in his encyclopedic classic entitled *The National Parks*. Tilden, however, could not finish his tribute to the park without mentioning its famous symbol. "Outstanding, naturally," he noted, "is that noble old-time resident, the Rocky Mountain bighorn."

Certainly, scouting for elk and bighorn sheep is the top draw for many wildlife watchers, but please read the chapters about these species carefully and familiarize yourself with the rules of etiquette for observing all wildlife. The feeding and harassment of wildlife have become chronic problems in Rocky Mountain, due primarily to the growing numbers of park visitors. By setting an example for your children and other visitors, you help pass on the tradition of wildness in Rocky Mountain to future generations.

From the crowning summit of Longs Peak at 14,255 feet above sea level to the lush blankets of willow that cloak the Colorado River, topography dictates where and when the best wildlife watching will occur. Besides the glacier-scoured mountains themselves, the most influential feature is an invisible line—the Continental Divide—that bisects the park from north to south. Some have called the Divide "the backbone of America," but it is more than a metaphor. It is actually a terrestrial precipice dictating whether rivers flow east toward the Atlantic Ocean or west to a terminus at the Pacific. Generally, the climate is moister west of the divide and drier east of it.

Why is this important to the wildlife watcher? In the park's wetter regions, there is a greater chance of locating the swamps and lush riverbottoms that attract moose, beavers, otters, waterfowl, and certain species of songbirds. To the east, in the more arid terrain, look for animals like mule deer, coyotes, ground squirrels, and cottontail rabbits, which thrive in drier conditions.

Another factor to consider is the season in which you visit. During spring, large migratory animals such as elk move to higher elevations, passing through certain migration corridors that are visually accessible to wildlife watchers. Throughout the summer, however, these animals graze on succulent grasses both below and above treeline, so roads that traverse higher elevations will produce better results. By autumn, when heavy snows begin falling, elk leave their isolated hamlets and descend to lower-elevation winter ranges that offer an abundance of forbs and twigs.

Visitors who want to taste the tropics need only spend a short time traveling across Rocky Mountain before they spot colorful birds that spend their summers in the park yet travel thousands of miles every year to winter in the jungles of Central and South America, Mexico, and the Caribbean. Over 200 species of birds have been identified in Rocky Mountain, and more than half are long-distance, neo-tropical migrants. Other birds, such as the federally protected bald eagle, stop in the park seasonally as they pass between nesting sites in Canada and winter destinations in the southern U.S.

For decades humans—like many birds—have been migrating seasonally into the hinterlands of the park, in search of one form of sustenance or another. Even Pope John Paul II sought Rocky Mountain's solitude during a pilgrimage to the U.S. Perhaps the most enduring description of Rocky Mountain's value to all citizens of the world was written by Enos A. Mills, who is considered the John Muir of Rocky Mountain National Park.

"This is a beautiful world, and all who go out under the open sky will feel the gentle, kindly influence of nature and hear her good tidings," Mills enthused in his 1909 classic, *Wild Life on the Rockies*. "Enter the forest, and the boundaries of nations are forgotten. It may be that some time an immortal pine will be the flag of a united and peaceful world."

A WILDLIFE WATCHER'S CODE OF CONDUCT

As a national park, Rocky Mountain is the domain of wildlife. Humans are merely guests. The ethics of responsible wildlife watching should always be observed, but they become even more important during winter months, when animals are strained by the bitter cold and the lack of available food. They are living off limited fat reserves that are crucial if they are to survive until spring. Those who approach a roadside animal and spook it into fleeing may be inadvertently hastening the animal's death. But no matter what the time of year, here are some basic tenets of responsible wildlife watching that should be observed:

Never feed wildlife

Wildlife in Rocky Mountain are far better off without human generosity. Throwing human foods to animals may lead to dependency upon unnatural snacks; in addition, the practice often makes the animal more aggressive and dangerous. This can result in injuries to park visitors and removal of the animals. Each year, park officials are forced to destroy a coyote or a member of another species because the individual has become habituated to handouts or has become so aggressive that it wanders into traffic. If visitors had followed the rules of proper wildlife, the animal's life would have been spared.

Maintain a safe viewing distance

Park regulations strictly forbid humans from leaving their cars and invading the space of wildlife. Not only is harassing wildlife prohibited in the park, but violators are subject to a fine. If an animal must alter its normal behavior due to your presence, you're too close. When you invade a wild animal's space, you may be disrupting the courtship of elk during the autumn rut, causing a federally protected peregrine falcon to leave its nest, or perhaps frightening a bighorn sheep into fleeing the roadside, thus forcing it to expend vital energy that it needs in order to survive through the winter.

Although many of the larger animals appear docile or tame, they can quickly become dangerous if they feel threatened. Mother animals with young are particularly sensitive to humans who intrude upon their comfort zone. The same rules apply to birds.

Never advance toward bird nests, because human disturbance of a site encourages abandonment of the nest by parents, and this in turn may trigger predation by coyotes or other carnivores.

These concerns take on even greater meaning during winter months, when animals are stressed by the cold weather and the deep snowpack. When Rocky Mountain is covered in a blanket of snow, hungry wildlife must forage harder for food. By approaching a roadside animal and spooking it, you may inadvertently hasten its death. For a closer view, use a zoom camera lens, a pair of binoculars, or a spotting scope.

Drive slowly and cautiously

The speed limits in Rocky Mountain are posted to ensure your safety and the safety of wildlife. Observe the reduced speed limits of 25, 35, or 45 miles per hour. Animals may cross the roadway at any moment, but motorists should be particularly alert around dawn and dusk, when many of the larger mammals are most active. In any case, driving slower creates better viewing opportunities, because the subtle presence of certain species is often difficult to detect at high speed. If you stop to take a photograph, try to find park pull-overs, especially on Trail Ridge Road and the Old Fall River Road, where your vehicle may cause damage to alpine tundra plant communities. Be aware that it is illegal to park in ditches along all national park roads. The most effective way of reducing traffic congestion in the park is to carpool.

Keep a clean camp

All food should be properly stored. Many dangerous encounters between people and wildlife could have been averted if the victims had maintained a clean campsite and stored their provisions properly. By failing to keep your food (including scraps, garbage, and left-overs) beyond the reach of animals, you're threatening your own safety and the safety of those who use the campsite after you've departed. If you decide to camp at a roadside site in the park, store your food in containers that prevent odors from escaping. The best place for food storage is in the trunk of a car. If you're camping in the backcountry, hang your food in a tree with a rope, but make sure it is stowed inside of a container that cannot be penetrated by bears, birds, or other animals. Hang the food at least 15 feet off the ground, over a tree limb that cannot easily be reached by a bear.

Avoid cooking smelly foods that may attract scavengers such as skunks or raccoons, and never sleep in the clothes you wore while cooking.

Finally—and this is perhaps the most important part of responsible camping—remember that all trash should be packed out of the backcountry or thrown away in garbage cans. Bring out everything that you brought in.

Restrain your pets

Pets—particularly barking or unruly dogs—are a liability to wildlife watchers. By their simple presence, pets are likely to frighten the animals that you and others hope to observe. In addition, pets can cause animals such as bears, mountain lions, and coyotes to exhibit aggressive behavior. Park regulations stipulate that all domestic animals must be under the owner's control and on a leash at all times. Pets are not allowed in the backcountry. If you have a choice, you're advised to leave your pet at home.

Leave antlers where you find them

It is illegal to remove antlers or horns found inside the national park. They are an important source of nutrients for many smaller mammals, and they serve as poignant reminders of the life and death cycle that continually occurs in all wild areas. Rocky Mountain contains both horned and antlered animals, but the only horned animals in the park are male and female bighorn sheep. Horns, composed primarily of keratin, remain permanently attached to a sheep's head throughout its life. The animals that grow deciduous antlers include male elk, moose, and mule deer. Although the antlers are shed during the winter months, new branches grow throughout the spring and summer.

Do not use artificial calls or spotlights

Park regulations forbid visitors from using artificial devices or vocal mimickry to lure wildlife, and also forbid trying to "shine" animals with spotlights. If you see other visitors using calls or spotlights, you're asked to report the activity to rangers at once.

WILDLIFE ENCOUNTERS

Here's a chart estimating the likelihood that you will encounter various species of wildlife within Rocky Mountain National Park. You may want to check off each species you're able to spot in the park.

Common: On any given day, you stand a good chance of encountering one or more of this species.

Irregular: By simply driving through the park without any information, you may see these species on chance encounters. However, by using the tips and suggested locations in this book, you improve your chances of seeing the animal.

Rare: While these animals have been seen in the park, they are spotted so rarely that it's impossible to predict whether you'll encounter the species.

MAMMALS	Common	Irregular	Rare
Bighorn Sheep		X	
Elk	X		
Mule Deer	X		
Moose		X	
Black Bear			X
Mountain Lion			X
Bobcat			X
Coyote	X		
Red Fox			X
Badger			X
River Otter			X
Beaver		X	
Porcupine		X	
Raccoon		X	
Striped Skunk		X	
Muskrat		X	
Yellow-Bellied Marmot	X		

MAMMALS	Common	Irregular	Rare
Pika	X		
Abert's Squirrel	X		
Red Squirrel	X		
Golden-Mantled Squirrel		X	
Pine Marten		X	
Weasel		X	
Snowshoe Hare		X	
Nuttall's Cottontail		X	

BIRDS	Common	Irregular	Rare
Golden Eagle		X	
Bald Eagle			X
Peregrine Falcon		X	
Red-Tailed Hawk	X		
White-Tailed Ptarmigan		X	
Water Pipit		X	
Black-Billed Magpie	X		
Gray Jay	X		
Raven	X		
Clark's Nutcracker	X		
Steller's Jay	X		
Western Tanager		X	
Mountain Bluebird	X		
Broad-tailed Hummingbird	X		
Blue Grouse		X	
American Dipper	X		
Common Snipe		X	
Mallard	X		

TIPS FOR FINDING WILDLIFE

▶ The most important factors that will affect your watching are the time of year and the time of day. Read each section about the species in which you are interested; then scout our recommended locations. Many animals within Rocky Mountain are nocturnal (night foraging) or crepuscular (most active at dawn and dusk). As a result, early morning and evening hours are often the most productive times for embarking on visual safaris. At high noon, your prospects are poor.
▶ Know the tools for safe wildlife watching. Your vehicle is the safest place you can be when bears and other large mammals are near the roadside. Instead of stepping closer to an animal, consider using a pair of binoculars, a spotting scope, or a long camera lens.

Spotting scopes are versatile because they can be mounted on a tripod or the window of a car. Particularly effective for viewing elk, bighorn sheep, moose, and mule deer, spotting scopes are occasionally set up by park rangers at turnouts in order to assist visiting wildlife watchers.

Don't underestimate the value of using your vehicle as a blind. Most large mammals and many bird species have learned to tolerate cars along the roadside as long as visitors stay inside of them.

Mike Francis (who took the photographs you'll find in this guide) recommends that amateur photographers add a 50-300mm zoom camera lens to their equipment bag if possible. "A 300mm is a solid lens that allows visitors to get sharp portraits without having to move in too close," he advises. "The lens most commonly used by my colleagues, though, is a 400mm." Visitors carrying cameras of any sort (including video cameras) should be advised that the rules of responsible wildlife watching apply equally to photographers.

PARK WILDLIFE IN BRIEF

▶ Several wildlife species that resided in or near Rocky Mountain National Park within recent times are now extinct in the area. The list includes the grizzly bear, the gray wolf, the bison, and the antelope.

▶ River otters, native to the park, were recently restored here; moose, non-natives, were introduced to wildlands adjacent to the Kawuneeche Valley. They have since begun colonizing the park along the Colorado River.

▶ After the peregrine falcon was extirpated from most of the West during the 1950s and early 1960s due to the use of DDT, the bird was reintroduced to the park.

▶ Many members of Rocky Mountain's thriving elk population are descendants of animals that were trapped and relocated several decades ago from the vicinity of Yellowstone National Park in Wyoming. Rocky Mountain may someday be considered as a site for wolf restoration. However, as of this writing, there are no plans to return the park's largest historic carnivore, the grizzly bear, to its former haunts.

▶ There are no poisonous snakes in Rocky Mountain National Park. Due to the high elevation, the garter snake is the park's only reptile, and it is non-poisonous.

▶ There are 147 lakes within the park, but only about 50 contain reproducing populations of fish. Ask a ranger which lakes are fishable and which regulations apply. A valid Colorado fishing license is required for all persons age 15 or older. There are five species of trout in the park—brown, brook, rainbow, greenback cutthroat, and Colorado River cutthroat. The native greenback cutthroat, which is on the federal endangered species list, is one of the rarest species in the Colorado Rockies. It is native only to the eastern half of the park. Anglers must return greenbacks to the water.

THE GREAT DIVIDE

The Continental Divide is more than an arbitrary line placed on a map of Rocky Mountain National Park. This topographical feature has an important effect on how much rain falls and which plant and animal communities are present. Here are some illustrations for wildlife watchers to consider:

CONTINENTAL DIVIDE

WEST SIDE	EAST SIDE
No glaciers	Glaciers
Colorado River trout	Greenback cutthroat trout
Moose	No moose
Colorado River and headwaters	No major river
No ponderosa pine	Ponderosa pine
25 inches annual moisture	13 inches annual moisture
Little wind	Windy
No Abert's squirrels	Abert's squirrels
River otter	No otter
No wood lily	Wood lily
No prickly pear cactus	Prickly pear cactus
Cold winters	Mild winters

Source: National Park Service

BEGINNING YOUR ADVENTURE: FOUR SUGGESTED ROUTES

It's best to think of your wildlife watching adventure not as a search for a single species, but as a visit to different communities of animals where topography and climate mold the population. Here are four recommended drives and the species you are likely to encounter.

TRAIL RIDGE ROAD —

Trail Ridge Road runs at an elevation of more than two miles above sea level. It is the navigational centerpiece of Rocky Mountain National Park (although closed in winter), and it is the main overland road connecting the community of Estes Park with the small resort town of Grand Lake. This paved route (Highway 34) climbs 4,000 feet in elevation, crosses the Continental Divide and, over the course of 50 miles, passes through several different ecosystems. It allows visitors to experience the dramatic differences between the wetter western half of the park and the drier eastern half.

Trail Ridge delivers what few national scenic roads in the lower 48 states can offer—a close-up view of alpine tundra from the comfort of a car. At first glance, the tundra appears stark and barren, but closer examination reveals a crazy quilt of color, especially during the summer after the snow has melted. Most importantly, it serves as a refuge for many plants and animals that have adapted over centuries to this high-elevation environment.

If you allow yourself a half-day or more and get an early start, it's likely that you'll spot elk and mule deer in the open meadows, plus a host of medium-sized and small mammals including coyotes, pikas, marmots, ground squirrels, and possibly a badger. Birders have excellent opportunities to see avian inhabitants, including golden eagles, red-tailed hawks, ptarmigan, water pipits, rosy finches, mountain bluebirds, and several different members of the crow family, including gray and Steller's jays, ravens, black-billed magpies, and Clark's nutcrackers. Below the treeline in the montane and subalpine forests, look for mountain chickadees and white-breasted nuthatches. In the aspen groves, you may locate warbling vireos and red-naped sapsuckers.

The Alpine Tundra Trail just west of Rock Cut is an excellent place to stretch your legs and scan the horizon with binoculars. Remember to stay on the trail at all times, because intrusion into the alpine tundra can cause damage to sensitive plants. Tread lightly.

FALL RIVER ROAD —

The paved road between the Fall River Entrance Station and the Endovalley picnic area is easily one of the country's premier areas for viewing bighorn sheep and elk during autumn. It's also a paradise for seeing other wildlife. At Sheep Lakes, which marks the beginning of Horseshoe Park, there is a good possibility of spotting sheep (May through July), elk, mule deer, coyotes, yellow-bellied marmots, red-tailed hawks, and mountain bluebirds. Farther west, in the forested alluvial fan and open meadow country that characterizes Horseshoe Park, look along the Fall River for dippers, many species of wood-peckers, and beavers. Focus on the rockpiles and trees to identify pikas, Steller's jays, and magpies. Once you reach Endovalley, motorists (during July, August, and early September) can continue for nine miles along the Old Fall River Road, a one-way gravel route that emerges at the Alpine Visitor Center. This area is one of the true hidden treasures for wildlife watchers, because it affords views of the alpine tundra found nowhere else. Most of the alpine tundra species that can be seen along Trail Ridge Road are also found here.

BEAR LAKE ROAD —

The Bear Lake Road, which winds into the mountains between the Moraine Park Museum and the Bear Lake Trailhead, is heavily traversed by people from the front range of the Rockies who know how spectacular the scenery is. Waterfalls, remnant glaciers, and several backcountry lakes are within reach from hiking trails along this road. In spite of the fact that Bear Lake Road becomes a busy place, it's a splendid destination; hikers here will find flat ground, and a few of the trails are accessible to handicapped visitors.

Motorists are urged to park their vehicles at Glacier Basin Campground and hop a shuttle bus that stops at most trailheads en route to Bear Lake. Utilizing the bus frees parents from the some-times maddening responsibility of driving while simultaneously try-ing to mind the kids; it also helps minimize traffic congestion and reduces human impact on the environment. By taking the early or late shuttles, fortunate wildlife watchers may see a black bear or a mountain lion crossing the road. Other, more commonly viewed animals include elk, deer, coyotes, magpies, ravens, pine martens, marmots, blue grouse, dark-eyed juncos, gray jays, mountain bluebirds, and western tanagers.

KAWUNEECHE VALLEY —

The portion of Highway 34 that traverses the Kawuneeche Valley west of the Continental Divide is a worthwhile wildlife safari all its own. Generally, the Kawuneeche Valley sees far fewer visitors than other areas. The wildlife watching opportunities, however, are tremendous. Here the climate is wetter and cooler; the mountainsides are more heavily forested; and the Colorado River drainage adds a dimension that is lacking on the other side of the park. Along the river between the Kawuneeche Visitor Center and the Colorado River Trailhead, you may see a moose, black bear, elk, mule deer, or coyote. Scan the willow bottoms for beavers, river otters, common snipe, black-headed grosbeaks, yellow warblers, and broad-tailed hummingbirds. Birding in the vicinity of Never Summer Ranch is exceptional. Perhaps you'll even be fortunate enough to see a northern harrier coursing across a meadow or an osprey diving to snatch a brook trout from the Colorado River. As you climb to Trail Ridge Road through the spruce and fir forest, keep your eyes open for blue grouse and pine grosbeaks.

WINTER ROADS —

The Highway 36/34 Loop and Bear Lake Road are open to auto travel in winter. Trail Ridge Road from Timber Lake Trailhead to Many Parks Curve is closed beginning with the first major snows of autumn until Memorial Day weekend. Old Fall River Road is open only from early July until September. Two visitor centers—the Headquarters Visitor Center near the town of Estes Park and the Kawuneeche Visitor Center on the west side of the park—are open daily during business hours.

MAMMALS
The BIGHORN SHEEP
Peak Performer

Bighorn sheep reign as the symbol of Rocky Mountain National Park. Indeed, the profile of a sheep perched upon a rock ledge is a breathtaking sight. By foot and by auto, scores of park visitors make pilgrimages into the alpine tundra each year to savor a peek at these true peak dwellers.

Bighorns (*Ovis canadensis*) inhabit the upper limits of Rocky Mountain's terrestrial landscape in ramparts largely free of trees and predators, yet continually subjected to inclement weather. Some 800 bighorns live in the park during all or part of the year.

The renewed growth of Rocky Mountain's sheep population is a conservation success story. Thousands of bighorns lived here during the 19th century, but by the early 20th century their numbers had declined to perhaps 150. Since then, however, aided by reintroduction efforts, the sheep population has rebounded to its current level.

Although bighorns move between wind-blown grasslands and natural salt licks, those that inhabit the park today are not nearly as peripatetic as their ancestors, animals that moved seasonally over great distances between the higher and lower elevations. In fact, most sheep in the park today remain in the high country all year. Generally, a coat of heavy hair allows them to endure temperatures that fall to -35 degrees Fahrenheit or even colder.

In contrast to elk, moose, and deer, both sexes of bighorn sheep grow horns that stay on their heads for life. While the C-shaped spirals that grow from the heads of male bighorns are better recognized and reach full curl at eight years of age, females have horns rising like straight spikes eight to ten inches long. Nannies bear a strong resemblance to mountain goats. Although non-native mountain goats have been advancing upon the park boundaries from areas in which they have been relocated for hunting purposes, park officials say they will do everything possible to prevent goats from colonizing the park, because they would compete with bighorns for rangeland. In addition, goats are classified in Rocky Mountain National Park as

an exotic species. It is unlikely, therefore, that visitors will ever have the opportunity to confuse bighorns with the yellowish-white mountain goats.

A bighorn is brownish-tan, with a white rump patch and whitish coloration around its nose. It has a stout, muscular frame that allows it to sprint across steep slopes and crags with a low center of gravity. Both sexes of bighorns tend to be larger than their mountain goat counterparts. Bighorns weigh between 125 and 300 pounds. A sheep's hooves are critical to its survival. The hooves are hard-edged, yet each one has a soft sole that provides traction. The sharp edges can be used an as effective weapon against mountain lions that try to ambush bighorns as they move from winter to summer ranges. Bestowed with keen eyesight and good hearing, sheep are timid animals that maintain a distance between their bands and other alpine tundra intruders.

Rams roam separately except during the breeding season, which usually occurs in December. With it comes a dramatic, head-butting lesson in wildlife behavior. Mature rams face off and crack their horns in a test of dominance at speeds of up to 40 miles per hour. The sound of colliding horns can be heard up to a mile away.

The winner earns the right to mate with ewes that give birth to lambs about 5-1/2 months later, usually in June. The sociable female sheep congregate in small herds, which makes them easy to locate in the spring and summer, when they form nursery bands to raise their lambs. The group is led by an elder matriarch.

After bighorns feed themselves on grasses, they can often be seen resting and simply chewing their cud. Although it's not uncommon to find rams grazing near ewes and their lambs, males band together and roam across ridgetops at still higher elevations.

The premier location for viewing sheep is Horseshoe Park. "During late spring and summer, bighorn sheep descend from the alpine areas of the Mummy Range into the meadows of Horseshoe Park, around Sheep Lakes," according to park literature. "Here, they graze and eat soil to obtain minerals not found in their high mountain habitat. The minerals are essential in restoring nutrient levels depleted by the stresses of lambing and a poor-quality winter diet." However, the information adds that the sheep experience stress when they attempt to cross Highway 34 on the north side of Horseshoe Park; that stress may reduce their resistance to disease.

Healthy bighorns are relatively long-lived, reaching documented ages of at least 15 years. According to park officials, the primary cause of mortality is not avalanches or predation from animals such as coyotes and mountain lions, but diseases—including lungworm, which can lead to pneumonia.

Poaching of rams has been a chronic problem in public wildlands throughout the West. Although hunting is forbidden in the park, visitors can help rangers by reporting any suspicious activity to park officials.

Where to Find Bighorn Sheep —
Fortunately for wildlife watchers, bighorn sheep are most active during the daylight hours.

▶ One of the best areas for viewing sheep in Colorado is Horseshoe Park, near the natural salt licks at Sheep Lakes along Highway 34. However, do not enter the "Bighorn Crossing Zone" with your vehicle or on foot when sheep are present. Also, park officials advise observers to stay by the roadside when sheep are in the meadow at Sheep Lakes. This area is used as both a summer and winter range. However, during the summer months, most sheep ascend to higher elevations, so bring along a spotting scope or binoculars. Feeding bighorns is prohibited and punishable by a fine.

▶ If you have the time, a hike from Bear Lake Trailhead along the Flattop Mountain Trail to the summit of Flattop Mountain at 12,234 feet has produced sheep sightings in the summer. Bring binoculars, but stay on the trail. Sheep as well as the alpine tundra environment are sensitive to disturbance.

▶ During winter months, bighorns can be seen just outside the park's Fall River Entrance Station along Highway 34, where members of the Black Canyon sheep population descend to lower elevations.

▶ Locations west of the Continental Divide that involve some hiking are "the Crater" area of Specimen Mountain, off Trail Ridge Road at Milner Pass. This trail is closed during the spring lambing season in May and June. Other viewing spots include Box Canyon and Skeleton Gulch in the Never Summer Range.

The ELK (WAPITI)
Bullish Bugler

Every autumn, the valleys of Rocky Mountain National Park erupt with the color of aspen and the sounds of "natural jazz." The park's crisp air is filled by bugling bull elk trying to herd cows into their harem. This time of year, which also involves fascinating displays, is known as the rut. For park visitors, few acts of animal behavior are as dramatic to observe. Rocky Mountain is considered one of the finest elk viewing places in Colorado.

The elk (*Cervus elaphus*) is the most abundant member of the deer family in Rocky Mountain, though not long ago the wapiti's

presence in the park had been eliminated. Once a species ranging from the Pacific Northwest to the Appalachians, the elk was completely extirpated from the East and most parts of the West—including Colorado—as a result of overhunting and habitat loss earlier in this century.

During the latter half of the 19th century, human settlement in the Estes Valley caused elk numbers to decline precipitously. Within two decades, elk were virtually extinct locally, and it wasn't until 1913—two years before the national park was established—that efforts were made to repopulate the high country with wapiti. The term *wapiti* is a Shawnee Indian description of the animal that means "white rump."

In 1913 and 1914, 49 elk captured in the vicinity of Yellowstone National Park were transplanted into Rocky Mountain. Ironically, the transfer accompanied a federal campaign to eliminate the elk's primary predators, gray wolves and grizzly bears. While the elk population rebounded (it currently numbers between 3,000 and 4,000 animals), the annihilation of wolves and grizzlies from the park hampered nature's ability to keep wildlife populations in check. Some biologists argue that the current problematic grazing by elk of tree species such as aspen could be eliminated by the presence of wolves. Today, the elk's primary natural enemy is the mountain lion, which preys on young calves; however, efforts may someday return wolves to Colorado and to Rocky Mountain National Park.

The health of the park is dependent upon protection of habitat both inside and outside of its boundaries. While about 1,500 elk stay in the national park year-round, another 3,000 or so migrate outside of Rocky Mountain to winter grasslands at lower elevations. Elk cannot survive without sufficient habitat, and development on private land along the national park's border continues to whittle the amount of critical rangeland needed by elk during the harsh winter months. One group that is working with the National Park Service and the U.S.Forest Service to preserve habitat is the Rocky Mountain Elk Foundation.

Mature elk are the second-largest animals in Rocky Mountain. Bulls weigh between 500 and 1,000 pounds, and they stand five feet tall or higher at the shoulders. Cows weigh between 400 and 600 pounds. The pelage of an elk is unmistakable, and is quite different from the grayish coat of a mule deer.

An elk's head is dark brown. The bulk of its body is tan, and the rump area is creamy white. A good indicator of elk presence is their tracks, which can be seen in mud or snow. The imprint resembles cloven half moons roughly four inches in diameter and rounder than moose tracks. Elk are found in all areas of Rocky Mountain, while moose inhabit only the Kawuneeche Valley in the western half of the park. Elk are most active at night and during the twilight hours of dawn and dusk. Summer travelers who get an early start in the morning should scan the high country near the treeline for groups of elk grazing in the stunted alpine forests known as krummholz stands, or in mountain meadows sloping away from roads.

Autumn triggers frenetic hormonal changes within the elk, particularly among polygamous bulls vying to mate with cows. A single bull may recruit a dozen or more cows into his harem, but only after he has displayed his dominance over numerous male challengers. The rut begins in late summer and lasts through the first weeks of November. It is announced when bulls emit high-pitched bugles that can be heard from miles away. Feverish jousting takes place as the bulls lock antlers, using their sharpened tines as offensive (and defensive) tools.

In recent years, the spectacle has attracted large crowds and caused concern among park biologists, who fear that humans might disrupt this important rite of autumn. As a result the Rocky Mountain Bugle Corps, comprised of concerned citizen volunteers, assembles in meadows at key viewing areas and instructs visitors in both natural history and the ethics of elk watching. When you're viewing bugling elk, always stay on the roadway or designated trails. Bulls are physically strained by the ordeal of the rut and can become aggressive, so humans should give them a wide berth.

As the rut ends, elk move from the high country to lower-elevation rangeland that provides enough accessible vegetation and browse to sustain them through the winter. Bulls begin dropping their antlers by March, and new growth begins almost immediately. Female elk do not sprout antlers.

In late May and June, pregnant cows retreat to solitary places in the forest, where they give birth to calves. Following delivery, mothers and calves come together in nursery bands, which feed and fend off predators together. At about this time, the bulls' new antler tines have reached a stage known as velvet. The term describes the soft surface of emerging antlers, nourished by blood vessels and capillaries. The branches eventually harden, and bulls rub off the velvet overcoating in time for the rut. Over the span of their 140-day development, antlers grow at a rate of about 1/2 inch per day, eventually reaching weights of up to 50 pounds.

The size of the antlers can help determine an animal's age. As a general rule of thumb, bulls between two and five years old carry racks with only a couple of tines on either side. From the fifth year through the age of nine, bulls often sport six tines on each side. In the West, such an elk is considered a six-point bull; however, observers east of the Mississippi River count the number of tines on both sides and declare it a 12-point bull. Wildlife photographers sometimes use artificial elk calls as a means of summoning bulls into view, but the practice is prohibited in national parks.

Proceed with caution if you see an elk near the roadway, and never walk up to animal that's grazing near your car. Cows are extremely protective of their calves, and bulls have been known to charge humans. Even though elk may appear docile and tame, never try to feed them. These animals are large, wild, and powerful. They can be extremely dangerous. Park regulations require that people who are outside of their vehicle must maintain a minimum distance of 25 yards from elk.

Where to Find Elk —

▶ During the autumn rutting season, the Rocky Mountain Bugle Corps is ready to assist park visitors who want to observe elk bugling at Horseshoe Park, Moraine Park, and Upper Beaver Meadows.

▶ West of the Continental Divide, an excellent place for listening to bugling bulls is the Kawuneeche Valley at dusk and dawn. The best strategy during September and October is to simply pull your car over at a designated turnout or campground between the Grand Lake Entrance Station and the Colorado River Trailhead. Turn off the engine, get out of the car, and enjoy an amazing natural soundtrack.

▶ In the spring and summer months, elk are often observed nightly in the high meadows visible from Trail Ridge Road.

▶ Wildlife watchers in winter can usually find elk grazing in the meadows around Park Headquarters west of Estes Park and in Moraine Park. Elk are also frequent winter visitors to the town of Estes Park. Elk are highly stressed during the winter months, and any encroachment upon elk grazing areas can cause the animals to expend precious energy reserves. This in turn can lead to their death.

The MULE DEER
Western Wanderer

The mule deer of Rocky Mountain National Park occur in far fewer numbers than the park's famous elk, but visitors nonetheless stand an excellent chance of observing these ungulates. From the streets of downtown Estes Park to the overlooks along Trail Ridge Road, mule deer are plentiful. "Mulies" *(Odocoileus hemionus)* are somewhat larger relatives of the widely distributed white-tailed deer, which is found from the East Coast to interior areas of the American West. Visitors can expect to find mule deer in most of the areas inhabited by elk, but at slightly lower elevations. While the males of

both deer and elk sprout majestic antlers, it's easy to distinguish one species from the other. Mule deer weigh roughly a third as much as wapiti (males about 200 pounds, females 125 to 150 pounds), and there are key, corresponding differences in antler size, body shape, and color distribution.

The light brown, almost tan, hair of the mule deer is evident on its back and forehead during the summer, but the hair becomes grayish brown in winter. The truly distinctive features of the deer are the black-tipped tail protruding from a cream-colored rump, and conspicuous, dull white patches inside its long ears, across its muzzle, and below the chin. Males, called bucks, grow beautiful sets of antlers that are nearly symmetrical. The racks are shed in early winter and start to re-emerge a few months later.

A mule deer's frame is brawny, with muscles that carry the animal across steep inclines and habitat ranging from low-lying riverbottoms and dry sagebrush valleys to open, subalpine grasslands. Small bands of male deer will sometimes venture above treeline in mid to late summer.

Mule deer subsist on a year-round diet of brushy vegetation. Nomadic for much of the year, they sometimes assemble on winter ranges in a process known as "yarding up." The time of courtship known as the rut commences in late October and early November; it casts dominant males into vigorous jousts for the right to breed with females. In June, following a gestation period of about 200 days, does give birth to fawns—usually twins. Glands situated near the hooves on the female's hind legs emit an odor that allows fawns to recognize their mother by virtue of her smell. The primary predators of mule deer in the park are coyotes, bobcats, and mountain lions.

Like elk, mule deer move to high elevations in the early summer and return to lowland areas during the winter. Mule deer do most of their foraging at night, so the best time to go deer-watching is just after dawn and in the hours before dusk, although the deer may be seen at any time of day.

Where to Find Mule Deer —

Although mule deer may appear tame, never try to approach or feed them. They can be aggressive and dangerous. Park regulations require that people outside of their vehicle maintain a safe distance from the deer, so the animals can roam undisturbed. In some national parks, mule deer bucks have impaled visitors with their antlers and kicked them with sharp hooves. If you see others approaching deer, encourage them to back off; you'll be doing the animals (and the people) a favor.

▶ From late April until early November, look for small groups of mule deer between the northeastern park entrance at Fall River (Highway 34) and the picnic area at Endovalley. Visitors will find particularly good spotting opportunities at Sheep Lakes. Binoculars and spotting scopes afford excellent views.

▶ Another productive route that yields plenty of mule deer sightings is the Bear Lake Road between Moraine Park Museum and the Bear Lake Trailhead. Deer and elk watching are best during the summer and autumn months. The park provides a shuttle bus service that visitors are encouraged to use.

▶ A third route that offers good year-round deer-watching opportunities is Highway 34 as it winds through the Kawuneeche Valley between the Kawuneeche Visitor Center and Farview Curve. Deer can be seen browsing at the forest edge or along riverbottoms around dawn and dusk.

▶ During winter months, mule deer can be observed near Beaver Meadows, Mill Creek, and Moraine Park.

The MOOSE
Towering Transplant

 According to biologists, moose *(Alces alces)* were not native to the national park, and only recently began colonizing the park's western tier after a number of them were transplanted into the adjacent Arapaho National Forest in 1978. Still, it's hardly difficult to explain why moose have adapted so well to life in the Kawuneeche Valley. Lush with willow, aspen, and alder—the animal's favorite winter browse—this region offers choice habitat for the largest member of the deer family.

Moose command attention because of their massive, gangling bodies, and the bulls are easily identified by their marvelous palmate antlers, which are shed and re-grown every year. Both bulls and cows have a shoulder hump, an elongated snout, a bulbous nose, and a pendulous dewlap or fur "bell" that hangs beneath the chin. Bulls occasionally reach a towering seven feet at the shoulders; they can weigh as much as 1,000 pounds.

It is possible for park visitors to mistake a cow moose for a cow elk, but closer examination reveals clear-cut differences between the two animals. The cow elk is considerably smaller; its coat is a lighter brown; and female elk are more likely to be seen in groups.

Moose are almost always found in the vicinity of water. They have extraordinarily long legs, allowing them to wade comfortably though riverbottoms and marshes, continually nibbling on aquatic plants or leafy tree stems along the way. About 90 percent of a moose's diet is comprised of browse from willows, shrubs, and conifers. Willows, however, provide the chief form of nutritional sustenance, and these trees are common on the edge of beaver ponds.

Don't be fooled by the moose's reputation as a gentle giant. Solitary bulls forage by themselves for a reason. Be especially wary of bulls during the autumn rut, though this mating ritual is fascinating if watched from a safe distance. Cows with calves are notorious for chasing and occasionally injuring humans who venture too close.

As a display of their masculinity, rutting bulls stomp through meadows and flay grasses with their antlers. Adult bulls occasionally tangle as they vie for territorial dominance. Bulls drop their antlers in late winter, but new ones begin growing almost immediately. The sheen of an antler is created in summer, when bulls rub a soft layer of velvet off the hardening rack.

A healthy moose can live for 20 years, and it's not uncommon to see the same moose at the same wetland year after year. Park officials estimate that roughly 25 to 30 moose inhabit the park year-round or seasonally.

Where to Find Moose —
▶ Although moose have been sighted throughout the park, they are identified chiefly with the Kawuneeche Valley west of the Continental Divide along Highway 34, between Grand Lake and Farview Curve.

The BLACK BEAR
American Omnivore

 Black bears are the largest wild omnivores found in Rocky Mountain National Park. Subsisting on a natural diet of meat and plants, these bruins range across forests in lower and middle elevations. Biologists estimate that roughly 30 black bears inhabit the park. Although the bears rarely appear along the roadside, the animals attract a great deal of attention whenever they come into view.

As evidenced by their scientific name, *Ursus americanus*, black bears are the "American bear," the most widely distributed bear species on the continent. It's a mistake to associate black bears only with their stereotypical jet-black hues, for their coats come in colors ranging from black to blonde, chocolate, cinnamon, and reddish-brown. Visitors frequently mistake lighter-colored black bears for grizzly bears, their larger ursine cousins.

Until the early decades of the 20th century, black bears in fact shared the national park with grizzlies. Unfortunately, hunters and ranchers who were intent upon protecting their livestock killed the last grizzlies in the park. Because of the grizzly's aggressive nature, it is unlikely that the species will be returned to Rocky Mountain anytime soon.

The extirpation of grizzlies has heightened public awareness of black bears, which have distinctive physical features. Some—though not all—black bears have white markings on their bellies; most have brown muzzles. Adult boars weigh between 200 and 400 pounds; sows weigh 150 to 300 pounds.

The wildlife watcher can watch for signs indicating that bears have been in the vicinity. The most obvious sign is tracks. Black bears are "plantigrade," or flat-footed walkers, just like humans.

The impression of five toes is usually visible, but the paw print is wider than a human's footprint, and it usually contains claw marks in front of the toes. The tracks are generally no more than seven inches long.

Another sure indication of bear presence is scat (fecal droppings). Bear scat is tubular and often dark-colored, and it reflects the animal's diet. When bears are feeding on carrion, for example, the scat is firm and sometimes laden with bones or fur. However, the texture is diarrhetic (runny) when the animal nourishes itself on berries later in the summer.

Contrary to popular notions, black bears do not hibernate; They lie in a state of dormancy with reduced blood flow and a slowed metabolism, relying upon stored bodily fat for nourishment, but they can and do awaken at times during the long winter months.

Nature has provided black bears with a unique means of reproducing. Although sows and boars breed in early summer, development of the embryo is delayed until autumn, when the expectant mother enters her den. During dormancy, beginning in late November, between one and four (but usually two) fetuses grow in the mother's womb. Cubs are born toward the end of winter; they grow in the den from an initial weight of about 12 ounces to more than ten pounds by the time they see their first daylight in April. Cubs usually remain with their mother until their second summer, then begin to forage and den on their own. Like grizzlies, black bears are long-lived. Some have reached documented ages of 20 years.

Black bears are opportunistic scavengers that are not fussy about what they eat. They can be seen grubbing for insects, small rodents, grasses, plant roots, berries, fish, or meat from dead animals. It is essential that park visitors maintain a clean camp at all times and refrain from feeding bears, because habituation can lead to human injury and the destruction or removal of bears from the ecosystem. Feeding bears is illegal and punishable by a fine.

In one respect, black bears have a profound edge over grizzlies. Not only are they good swimmers, but they're highly adept at climbing trees. Sharp claws enable adult black bears and cubs to scale thin lodgepole pines as well as fir and ponderosa pines to escape danger. Females are fiercely territorial when protecting their cubs, so it's wise to announce your presence on a backcountry trail by making noise.

When provoked, black bears have been known to follow humans up a tree, which means it's important to avoid a confrontation.

Never approach a black bear, no matter how tame the animal appears. Remember that the bear is wild and dangerous. If you are away from the roadside and unable to get inside your car, stand your ground and make noise in an effort to scare the animal away. Try not to look the bear in the eyes. If the bear continues to approach, lay in the fetal position with your arms covering your face and neck.

Black bears are hunted outside of the national park in Colorado, but Rocky Mountain's prohibition on hunting affords the bears a year-round refuge. Still, poaching of bears to satisfy a global market for gall bladders, claws, and trophy heads has seriously imperiled several populations of black bears across the country. Citizens play a major role in the bear's protection, and any suspicious activity should be reported to park rangers.

Where to Find Black Bears —
▶ Look for black bears in more remote areas of the park, including Endovalley, Bear Lake, and Wild Basin. Park regulations specify that humans must remain at least 100 yards from bears. If you see other visitors inching closer to bears or tossing food, remind them that black bears are dangerous and that feeding animals does more harm than good.
▶ The best time to see black bears is in the early morning after sunrise or in the evening before sundown. However, they are most active during the night, when black bears move into meadows from the cover of forest.

The MOUNTAIN LION
Monochrome Cat

Mountain lions are North America's largest cats. The species name *(Felis concolor)* means literally "cat of one color" but these tawny-hued felines are known by many colloquial names, including cougar, puma, and catamount. In recent years, mountain lions have been seen with increasingly regularity throughout the Rockies, including suburban areas located in mountainous foothills.

An estimated 16,000 mountain lions inhabit mostly remote areas of the United States from the Pacific Northwest to the lower

Appalachians. Biologists speculate that an increased number of cats is one reason why more people have come in contact with the large predators in recent years, but there is no precise figure available for the number of mountain lions that range across Rocky Mountain National Park. At one time, cougars were stalked by federal bounty hunters intent upon eliminating all predators that posed a threat to livestock and game animals.

Although a mountain lion will rarely approach a park visitor, humans have good reason to respect these animals, as several people have been injured or killed in cat encounters over the past decade. Weighing between 75 and 200 pounds at adulthood, mountain lions in fact have no natural enemies except humans. Because they are equipped with long, retractable claws, they can climb trees as easily as they scale vertical cliffs. Agile and fleet, mature lions can leap nearly 20 feet in a single bound, and their favorite hunting method involves waiting in ambush. Mule deer are the main staple of their diet, but lions have also killed elk, bighorn sheep, porcupines, beavers, ground birds, and rabbits. Studies show that the average adult female and its young can subsist on roughly one mule deer per week.

Over the course of its nightly hunting sojourn, a mountain lion may travel a dozen or more miles along river drainages, through forests, and across rocky inclines and alpine meadows. The hours near sunrise and sunset are the best for cat watching, though any sighting is likely to be accidental.

Signs of mountain lion presence include copious scat ranging from dark spheres to pellets, often containing traces of whatever the lion ingested, such as deer hair or bones. Tracks, measuring between three and four inches in diameter, are wider than they are long. The imprint of four toes makes the tracks resemble those of a housecat.

Breeding takes place in late winter or early spring, and a litter of one to six kittens is delivered in early summer. Generally, young lions leave their mothers one to two years after birth and establish a solitary existence except during mating. Mountain lions maintain a den, but they do not hibernate. They are active all year, and their health is largely dependent upon the availability of prey.

Biologists speculate that many human-cat encounters involve sub-adult animals that are hungry and trying to establish their own territory. The recommended conduct when confronted with a curious lion is slightly different than what's recommended in a bear confrontation. Never run from a lion you meet in a campground or on a trail. Running triggers the predatory instinct in the lion, and the animal is likely to chase. Instead, act as aggressively as possible, perhaps shouting and waving your arms. Do not crouch or "play dead." If yelling fails to drive the lion away, consider using rocks or sticks to impede its advance.

Where to Find Mountain Lions —

Never approach a mountain lion. Visitors to Rocky Mountain should restrain their pets at all times, as dogs and cats have been known to attract mountain lions.

▶ Sightings of mountains lions have occurred in the vicinity of Horseshoe Park, along Bear Lake Road, and in the mountains overlooking the Kawuneeche Valley.

The BOBCAT
Wary Wildcats

 Like mountain lions, bobcats *(Felis rufus)* range across Rocky Mountain National Park. However, they are equally secretive and equally wary of humans. As a result, it is virtually impossible to predict when and where these cats will be seen.

Rocky Mountain sits in the middle of bobcat country, which extends from Mexico to the southern border of Canada. Bobcats, in fact, are the most widely distributed wildcat indigenous to the continent. As many as 1.5 million bobcats are believed to inhabit the U.S. They take their name from their classic stubby tails.

Bobcats are similar in appearance to lynx, but lynx are not found this far south in the Rockies. Bobcats weigh between 20 and 60 pounds and are quite adept at climbing trees, but you are just as likely to spot one walking in a rocky meadow or at the edge of the forest.

You can identify a bobcat, which resembles a brownish-gray tabby housecat, by the brownish spots on its coat, by the black tufts of hair that extend from the top of its ears, and by the knobby or "bobbed" tail, which is never more than five inches long. The coat turns gray during winter. Even when the animal isn't actually in view, you may encounter signs that a bobcat has been using the area. The bobcat's tracks and scat resemble those of a coyote.

The bobcat's favorite prey animals include snowshoe hares and Nuttall's cottontails, birds, and small rodents. It will often ambush its meal. During the day, bobcats lay low, often resting in a rock outcropping; at night, they begin their wandering, which can extend over many miles in a single evening.

Breeding takes place in late winter or early spring, and a litter of one to seven kittens (usually two or three) is delivered in May. Although bobcats are trapped and hunted for their fur outside of the park, they are afforded refuge from human harassment within Rocky Mountain. The population here is thought to be stable.

Where to Find Bobcats —

Dawn and dusk are the best times of day to scout the rocky ridgelines and forested edges for bobcats. Although sightings have occurred throughout the park, there is a heightened possibility of seeing them where there is an abundance of rabbits and hares. Such areas within the park include the Kawuneeche Valley and Bear Lake Road.

The COYOTE
Intrepid Trickster

The Native American tribes that once hunted in Rocky Mountain National Park revered the coyote as a mythological figure. The animal was known to many aboriginal peoples as "the singing trickster." Modern wildlife watchers regard these canid carnivores as a link to our primordial past.

When visitors sit around a campfire at night or pull their cars over and peer into the darkness, they often hear coyotes announcing their presence through song. Indeed, the yips and barks of coyotes *(Canis latrans)* are distinctive sounds of the wilderness that everyone should hear at least once. Fortunately, coyotes can be seen hunting their prey at many locations within the park.

Wildlife watchers routinely confuse coyotes with wolves. Since there are presently no wolves residing in Colorado, identification of coyotes becomes easier. As the year progresses, coyotes undergo color changes as a means of camouflage. In spring and summer, their pelage is brownish-red, though it turns gray as winter snows advance. Their undersides are usually white, regardless of the season. Coyotes resemble mid-sized dogs; they weigh between 20 and 30 pounds and have fluffy tails that point downward as the animal trots along.

Whether you're hiking down a trail or parked along the roadside, physical clues will let you know if a coyote has been using the area. The first clue is the scat (feces), which resembles a dog's and will often contain hair or bone fragments from the animal's last meal. Depending on the season, coyotes will scavenge or hunt for almost any available prey—rabbits, rodents, grasshoppers, carrion from deer, elk, moose, or bighorn sheep, the eggs deposited by ground-nesting birds, grouse, and sometimes even plants. Another indicator of coyote presence is their tracks, which look like a dog's but measure at least 2 1/2 inches long and are highlighted by four toe and claw imprints.

In spring, roughly two months after breeding, coyote females dig dens and give birth to between five and seven pups. Some coyote pairs stay together for years; the male hunts for the female as she nurses the young. The average lifespan of a coyote is about ten years.

Earlier in this century, federal wildlife officials tried to eradicate coyotes from Rocky Mountain because the wild canids posed a threat to livestock and game animals near the park's borders. However, coyotes are one of the most adaptable animals in North America. Unlike wolves, which were extirpated from most of their former range, coyotes prosper in both wilderness and suburban environments. They are found from the Atlantic to the Pacific; from serene sanctuaries like Rocky Mountain National Park to metropolitan areas such as Los Angeles and Denver. Although coyotes are still regarded as vermin in many parts of the West, where they occasionally prey upon domestic sheep, they are protected within the park.

In the absence of wolves, coyotes are the top dog of the canid food chain. In areas where coyotes are hunted, they are nocturnal (night-foraging). In Rocky Mountain they can be seen at any hour of the day, though the best times are dawn and dusk. Look for them on the edges of forest, in open meadows, and sometimes in the alpine tundra.

Where to Find Coyotes —

▶ Coyotes are regularly seen during the summer and autumn in the vicinity of Horseshoe Park along Highway 34 at dusk and dawn.

▶ Another prime viewing location is the alpine tundra along Trail Ridge Road, particularly at such overlooks as Forest Canyon, where coyotes hunt for marmots and pikas.

▶ Coyote sightings have been reported on Bear Lake Road between Sprague Lake and the Glacier Gorge Junction Trailhead.

▶ On the park's west side, listen for coyotes yipping in the evening hours from the Green Mountain Trailhead, the Bowen/Baker Trailhead, and the Colorado River Trailhead in the Kawuneeche Valley.

The RED FOX
Cosmopolitan Canid

Generally, the red fox *(Vulpes vulpes)* is considered a cosmopolitan species, because it occurs in Asia, Europe, and four-fifths of the North American continent. In Rocky Mountain National Park, however, sightings have been irregular at best. This canine predator is more common at lower elevations around the park's perimeter, particularly around ponds and open meadows, than it is in the center of the park. But visitors have seen red foxes both east and west of the Continental Divide.

Rarely does a wildlife watcher mistake a red fox for a coyote. For starters, foxes weigh one-third less than coyotes. In identifying a fox, remember that the species has a classic, billowing tail at least one-third the length of its body, culminating in a white tip. Although the majority of red foxes sport furry coats dominated by an orange-red (rust-colored) hue, color variations do occur. Foxes may be black, silver, or reddish-brown; however, biologists report that nearly all sightings within the park have involved red-phased animals.

Mating takes place in winter, and it's not uncommon for breeding red foxes to perform a "dance" by playfully standing on their hind legs and interlocking their front legs in a ritual of courtship. Fox kits are born blind, usually in an underground den almost two months after mating, but they gain vision and emerge from the den within about a month.

Like most carnivorous mammals, foxes possess a keen sense of smell. Their food staples include rabbits, mice, and birds, although they also eat berries and insects such as grasshoppers. Fox tracks, which feature four toes and claw marks, resemble a dog's prints; they're 2-1/2 inches or less from front to back.

Although red foxes are hunted and trapped outside the park, the animals are protected within Rocky Mountain. Here, free from human harm, they may be more active during the day than their counterparts elsewhere, but they remain most active as hunters during the night. The vast majority of sightings are documented during the early morning around sunrise and in the evening hours preceding dusk.

Where to Find Red Foxes —
▶ Red fox sightings have been reported between the Fall River Entrance Station and the picnic area at Endovalley, and along Highway 34 in the Kawuneeche Valley between the Onahu Creek Trailhead and Farview Curve. However, these canids are considered rare in Rocky Mountain National Park.

The BADGER
Bulldozing Burrower

 Badgers *(Taxidea taxus)* are nomadic burrowers that follow their primary sources of prey—ground squirrels and pocket gophers—as new rodent colonies spring up across Rocky Mountain's high open country. It is difficult to predict when and where sightings of badgers will occur, but a large hole in the side of a hill with plenty of disturbed earth constitutes evidence of their burrowing. And if you locate a thriving population of ground squirrels or gophers, it's likely that a badger will be nearby.

Badgers are best viewed from a distance, for they can be fiercely territorial and may charge intruders who venture too close to their dens. The markings on a badger's coat are striking; the design of its body is low to the ground but imposing. Look for a conspicuous line of white under the badger's snout, across its flattened head, and

along its upper backbone. The badger also sports a patch of white fur on both cheeks and ears, broken only by a hook-shaped pattern of dark brown. Most of its back is marbled gray and brown.

A carnivore with extraordinary strength for its size (it weights only 30 pounds), this scrappy member of the weasel family spends most of its life digging—carving out a new den with its long claws or bulldozing its way into a ground squirrel den for a meal.

Coyotes are one of the few rival predators tolerated by badgers; in fact, the two animals may develop a cooperative partnership. As a badger digs its way into the den of its prey, a coyote will sometimes wait with open mouth outside the den's alternate escape hatch. Despite the badger's habit of simply leaving its victims' bones and hair outside the den, it is fastidious about grooming its coat and buries its own scat.

Generally, badgers are nocturnal (night foraging), but due to the absence of human hunting inside the park, they can be seen at any time of day.

Where to Find Badgers —
▶ Scan the alpine tundra meadows along Trail Ridge Road at locations such as Medicine Bow Curve, Forest Canyon Overlook, Many Parks Curve, and Rainbow Curve, where populations of chipmunks, Wyoming ground squirrels, or pocket gophers are present.

The RIVER OTTER
Playful Paddler

Once nearly extirpated from most of the non-coastal West by fur trappers, river otters *(Lutra canadensis)* are now using the waters of Rocky Mountain National Park to regain a foothold in Colorado. Within the park, the species is found primarily west of the Continental Divide in the Kawuneeche Valley, but animals relocated from other parts of the country are successfully repopulating their home here. In the 1970s and 1980s, state wildlife officials turned 43 river otters loose in the Colorado River headwaters.

No creatures in Rocky Mountain are more delightful to watch than river otters. They are the second largest marine mustelid (member of the weasel family) in North America—only sea otters are bigger. Their long, slender frames are effectively water-dynamic. Using their furry tails as rudders, their webbed feet as propulsion aids, and their valve system to prevent water from entering the nostrils, river otters are excellent swimmers. They need considerable agility in order to catch trout, frogs, and other prey. River otters are protected from frigid waters by their thick, waterproof fur. Males, which grow to lengths of four feet, attain weights of about 25 pounds; females weigh slightly less.

Otters have special adaptations for reproduction. Although mating takes place in the spring, development of embryos (usually twins) is delayed until winter. The young are finally born in March or April, nearly a year after breeding took place.

Whether an otter is sliding down snowbanks or swishing through a calm stream, park wildlife watchers are charmed by the animal's playful nature. Two indicators of otter presence are five-toed tracks in the mud that usually reflect the animal's webbed feet, and greenish scat (fecal droppings) laced with fish bones or scales.

Making their home beneath a riverbank or the shoreline of a pond, otters dig permanent dens that are accessible through underwater lanes called "runs." Carved deeply into the bed of the stream, these passageways cannot freeze shut during winter, so otters are ensured a safe, year-round route between warm shelter and open water. River otters are active both day and night, and you're likely to see one if you simply sit by a river and wait quietly.

Where to Find River Otters —
▶ The lower Kawuneeche Valley, which cradles the Colorado River, houses a stable otter population. Watch the slower-moving sections of the river and willow thickets during morning and evening hours.

The BEAVER
Aggressive Architect

During the 19th century, beavers in the Colorado Rockies were nearly wiped out by fur trappers and Indians, who used the animal's pelts for trading. Today, the aggressive dam builders have made a comeback and are enhancing wildlife habitat in Rocky Mountain National Park.

A builder of wetland empires, the beaver *(Castor canadensis)* is a landscape architect whose backwater creations play an important role in ecosystems. By damming streams and thereby creating ponds, the beaver spawns habitat that benefits dozens of species. Willow, aspen, cottonwood, and alder trees thrive on the edge of a beaver's reservoir, providing an important source of browse for moose, elk, and deer. River otters, mink, and muskrats inhabit a beaver's slough, and ruffed grouse gather in the deciduous trees. Waterfowl, including mallard ducks, build their nests here, and birds such as snipe may

forage at the edge. All of this is visible to wildlife watchers who travel through the Kawuneeche Valley along the Colorado River and along other park waterways where beavers have established colonies.

With its resilient, bucked teeth, a beaver chews the trunk of a tree to a conical point, fells it, then uses the log as material for a dam or a spherical lodge. As the largest rodent in North America, the beaver is ideally adapted to water. It employs its flat, paddle-like tail to navigate in the water; its heavy, waterproof fur insulates the animal from the icy cold; and it has valves that prevent water from entering its nose and ears. Biologists regard the beaver as a constructive force in altering the environment, but there are some outside the park who resent the animal's ability to flood pastures or stop the flow of a creek so that water irrigating a field is cut off. In places where beavers are viewed as a nemesis to agriculture, they have been shot or removed. Within Rocky Mountain, they contend only with natural predators such as coyotes, bobcats, and red foxes, which will kill a beaver if they find it on land. Mink will actually enter beaver lodges and eat kits. If a beaver is startled by human presence, the animal will slap its tail down on the water and dive out of sight.

Where to Find Beavers —
Never approach or harass beavers. Give yourself and other visitors the pleasure of observing them as they naturally behave. They are most active at night, so the best hours for viewing them occur just before sundown and sunrise.

▶ Look for beavers along the Colorado River in the Kawuneeche Valley, particularly in the vicinity of Onahu Creek. Also watch for beaver presence at the ponds around Hidden Valley and upper Horseshoe Park.

▶ If you have time for a hike, you can observe beaver activity along the 2.3-mile Cub Lake Trail, found at the west end of Moraine Park.

▶ For an indication of what a beaver pond may become in the future, scan Beaver Meadows on the east side of the Continental Divide. The area was once a wetland.

The PORCUPINE
Prickly Plant-Eater

Porcupines can be spotted anytime and anywhere in Rocky Mountain National Park, but this timid, prickly-pear mammal—the only species of its kind in North America—prefers mostly to stay in the pine woodlands and willow thickets found at mid to lower elevations.

The porcupine *(Erethizon dorsatum)* is, of course, best known for its armor. An adult carries up to 30,000 spiny quills in its bodily quiver; however, contrary to popular belief, a porcupine cannot shoot its quills into an attacker. Rather, the quills are earned by any animal that puts an unwanted nose or paw into the porcupine's guard hairs. The quills are quite easily released from a porcupine's coat, but it is far more difficult to remove the sharp barbs from an impaled victim.

Wobbly in their slow gait, porcupines are surprisingly adept at scaling trees. They have soft underbellies and yellowish-brown guard hairs covering the quills on their backs. Their faces are non-menacing, and they generally mind their own business unless provoked. Well-nourished adult animals can attain weights of 35 to 40 pounds.

Male porcupines are solitary until the autumn mating period, when they join females and engage in high-pitched squealing during courtship. Following a gestation period of about seven months, one baby is born with a full set of quills that are soft at birth but harden within hours.

One sign of porcupine presence is their trademark paw prints, which look as if the bottoms of the feet were cobbled in pebbles. Marks from their long claws are usually visible also. Another sign of porcupine activity is a tree with its bark pulled away from the trunk and tooth marks left in place of the bark. Porcupines eat bark and complement their vegetarian diet with twigs, leaves, lupine, and other plants.

The animal also has a taste for salt that can become lethal. Rocky Mountain does not salt its roads in winter, but elsewhere many porcupines feeding on road salt are killed by passing automobiles. Predators of the porcupine in Rocky Mountain include coyotes, mountain lions, and bobcats. The average lifespan of a healthy adult is seven to eight years.

Where to Find Porcupine —

If you spot a porcupine, make certain that your pet is under control. It may suffer painful injuries inflicted by quills if it attempts to chase the porcupine. Because porcupines are primarily nocturnal, they are spotted most often in the early morning hours along roads or in meadows before they retreat into the forest. Drive with caution, as they often cross roads within the park.

▶ It is difficult to predict where a porcupine might be sighted, though frequent observations have been reported in the Kawuneeche Valley and along the Old Fall River Road. In recent years, wooden signs at the Alpine Visitor Center have also been gnawed by hungry porcupines.

The SNOWSHOE HARE
Winter Sprinter

The dedicated wildlife watcher may spot two members of the rabbit-hare family in Rocky Mountain National Park: the larger, better-known snowshoe hare and the Nuttall's cottontail.

The snowshoe *(Lepus americanus)* weighs between two and three pounds and is found on the west side of the park, where snowfall can be heavy. Its broad hind feet, which are four to five inches long, enable the snowshoe hare to move at sprinter's speed through forests that are difficult for many of the its predators to navigate. The snowshoe is also equipped with keen eyesight and hearing to help it detect intruders.

In summer the snowshoe's pelage is dark brown, accented by a white belly. In winter the body fur turns white to match the landscape and offers vital camouflage from its enemies, which include bobcats, foxes, mink, owls, and hawks.

The snowshoe is famous for its wide populations swings, which are cyclical and seem to occur at intervals of a decade—sometimes affecting the abundance of animals that prey upon them. In Canada, for example, the lynx population closely parallels the increases and decreases in the number of hares.

A female snowshoe may have several litters over the course of a year, but a high number of the young will die before the end of their first year of life. Snowshoes feed primarily on grasses, fruit, and aspen leaves during the summer; in winter, they turn to the bark of deciduous trees and conifer buds. However, snowshoes are omnivorous, and many wildlife watchers are surprised to learn that snowshoes will eat meat if they are hungry enough.

You're most likely to see snowshoes during the early morning and evening hours. They tend to keep a low profile during the day, sleeping out of view in hollow logs or underground dens. The surest and most visible sign of snowshoe presence is their tracks. The twin prints of their hind feet actually occur in front of the round tracks left by the front paws. Southern Colorado and northern New Mexico represent the southernmost portion of the snowshoe hare's range.

Where to Find Snowshoe Hares —
▶ At dawn and dusk throughout the year, scan the forests in the Kawuneeche Valley for snowshoe hares.

The YELLOW-BELLIED MARMOT
Whistling Squirrel

The sight of yellow-bellied marmots is synonymous with the Rocky Mountain high country. These frumpy ground squirrels are popular roadside attractions at many of the scenic overlooks.

As its name implies, the yellow-bellied marmot *(Marmota flaviventris)* has a belly covered with yellowish fur, darker brownish-yellow fur on its back, a stubby, bushy tail of the same color, and whitish markings on the face and chin. A binocular view will reveal the animal's resemblance to the groundhog.

Yellow-bellies share their habitat with pikas. Both species prefer to set up a home inside rock piles or scree slopes, as these locales afford easy access to the kinds of grasses they eat. More importantly, the jumble of boulders provides cover used to evade predators.

When threatened, yellow-bellies retreat to a safe hiding place and begin emitting whistling sounds. This is at least part of the reason for colloquial nicknames bestowed on them such as "whistle pigs" and "rockchucks." When a predator is in the area, it's common to hear several marmots calling back and forth among the rocks. The primary enemies of marmots in Rocky Mountain National Park are coyotes, eagles, foxes, and badgers.

The viewing season for yellow-bellies is a short one, because marmots spend the majority of the year hibernating in their dens. In fact, autumn visitors to the park are not likely to see any yellows-bellies. After fattening up on grasses, marmots go underground beginning in early September and usually no later than early October. They remain in a sleep-like state in their burrows until the following April or May. Males and females breed shortly after they emerge from their dens, producing a litter after about a month of gestation.

Marmot activity is heaviest in the early morning and in the evening before dusk.

Where to Find Yellow-Bellied Marmots —
▶ Look for yellow-bellies seasonally near Rock Cut, Forest Canyon Overlook, near the Endovalley picnic area, and at Marmot Point along Old Fall River Road. Please don't feed marmots.

The ABERT'S SQUIRREL
Rabbit-Eared Rodent

Racing across the boughs of ponderosa pine, the Abert's squirrel (*Sciurus aberti*) brings colorful animation to the montane forests of Rocky Mountain National Park. This is the most handsomely ornamented squirrel in the park.

The dark gray hair on the back of the Abert's contrasts sharply with the squirrel's white underbelly. Yet what makes this rodent most recognizable is its furry tassel ears, which look like a rabbit's, and its bushy, grizzled gray tail. The park contains a significant population of Abert's squirrels that are melanized (dark black) in color, offering a striking counterpoint to the resident population of red squirrels. Abert's squirrels are roughly three times the size of red squirrels.

It's a treat to see an Abert's because the species is found only in certain portions of the central and southern Rockies. Within the park, the squirrel resides east of the Continental Divide in lower, arid lands that support the growth of ponderosa pine. The tree nourishes these squirrels, not only with cone seeds but with the cambium (inner bark layer) as well.

Abert's squirrels remain active throughout the winter. They build their nests out of sticks and grass in the crotch of a tree, using this as a base camp for foraging efforts. When winter conditions become severe, the squirrels venture out to a seed midden site (or cache) buried in the ground, then return to their arboreal dens.

Abert's squirrels spend most of their lives off the ground; binoculars will help you spot them in trees. An interesting ritual occurs during spring mating (March and April), when these males scurry in chattering pursuit after breeding females. A litter, usually numbering three or four, is born after gestation of about seven weeks. The offspring are blind and hairless, but they quickly gain their sight, and they acquire a hairy coat within two months. Hawks are primary enemies that can easily gain access to the squirrels' high-altitude hamlets.

Where to Find Abert's Squirrels —
▶ Look for Abert's squirrels in the ponderosa pine forest west of the alluvial fan along Highway 34 in Horseshoe Park. Never feed Abert's squirrels. A natural diet suits them far better than human handouts.

The PIKA
Vegetarian Ventriloquist

One of the most-watched mammals in Rocky Mountain National Park is no bigger than a mouse. The pika *(Ochotona princeps)* weighs only three or four ounces, yet its bleating attracts considerable attention.

This round-eared relative of the rabbit, only six to eight inches long and resembling a guinea pig, makes its home in high-elevation scree slops and rockslide areas that happen to coincide with some of the best roadside turnouts along Trail Ridge Road.

The pika (pronounced PIE-KUH) has reddish-brown fur, white paws, and no visible tail. It sounds a shrill, high-pitched bleat (or whistle) when threatened or when communicating with its own kind.

This sound accounts for one of its nicknames—"whistling hare." In Rocky Mountain, the vocalizations inform humans of pika presence; the noises also tip off birds of prey, coyotes, and weasels—the animal's main predators. But all is not as simple as it seems. The pika is a talented ventriloquist that can "throw" sounds away from its actual location, misleading its pursuers.

It seems hard to believe that ancestors of the pika migrated across the Bering Strait from Asia thousands of years ago, but evidence of this overland trek can be traced to the pika's name, which is derived from a Mongolian description.

In June and July, female pikas give birth to between two and six young following a 30-day gestation period. The babies are blind and hairless at birth, though in coming weeks they gain eyesight and their coat starts to grow. A female sometimes mates twice during a summer, giving birth to a second litter.

Pikas are vegetarians. They collect grasses and sedges that not only provide food for winter, but provide a warm bed deep in the rocks. Unlike marmots, pikas remain active during the winter, emerging from their subterranean dens to forage even during the coldest months. They are most active during daylight hours. Evidence of pika presence includes white or brownish urine squirts on rocks.

Where to Find Pikas —
▶ Look for them at several roadside turnouts along Trail Ridge Road, including Forest Canyon Overlook, Rainbow Curve, and Rock Cut.

BIRDS

The GOLDEN EAGLE
Soaring Speedster

Two vistas dominate a wildlife watcher's view in Rocky Mountain National Park: the earth, with its complement of terrestrial mammals; and the sky, which holds a half dozen species of raptors aloft in the wind. Given the park's rugged mountain walls, high open meadows, and abundant rodent populations, golden eagles here live in a rich environment.

Golden eagles *(Aquila chrysaetos)* are named for their "golden" (actually dark brown) head feathers; but what truly distinguishes them from bald eagles is that they hunt primarily over land, rather than water. These majestic birds of prey are an imposing presence in the sky as they soar with seven-foot wingspans and in a dive reach speeds of 100 miles per hour. By using their keen eyesight, equal to seven-power binoculars, and their incredible maneuverability, golden eagles can spot prey from hundreds of feet above the ground and dive down to snatch a rabbit, a small rodent, or even a fawn in their talons.

During the 1960s the number of golden eagles declined sharply, as did other raptor populations, primarily due to the widespread use of the pesticide DDT. Today the golden eagle population appears to have stabilized within the park, but the species remains protected under the International Migratory Bird Treaty.

When identifying golden eagles, look first to the color of the feathers, then to the head. In differentiating between goldens and immature bald eagles, which bear a striking resemblance to one another, consider the type of terrain. Bald eagles tend to congregate around water, while golden eagles inhabit country that is drier and more open. If you're traveling through Rocky Mountain and you spot a brown eagle, it's probably a golden.

From the ground, the outline of a golden eagle resembles that of a hawk. The adult golden's full brown plumage appears when the bird is about four years old, following two or three moltings (feather sheddings). Despite the raptor's reputation among sheep ranchers for killing young lambs, goldens will hunt wildlife such as ground squirrels, marmots, rabbits, and prairie dogs if sufficient prey is available.

During the spring breeding and nesting season, goldens demand solitude. They build their nests, called eyeries, out of sticks and twigs placed on a high rock ledge or at the top of a pine. The female generally lays two whitish eggs. Successful production of offspring, however, can be dependent upon the weather. Late blizzards and high winds have been known to take their toll on young birds before they're able to fledge. It's especially important to minimize human intrusion during the nesting season.

Where to Find Golden Eagles —
▶ Travel to Forest Canyon Overlook or Rainbow Curve on Trail Ridge Road; watch for eagles soaring high in the sky, hunting for ground squirrels or marmots over the meadows that angle away from the road.
▶ Drive to the Twin Owls Trailhead north of the town of Estes Park and, if you have time, hike the Black Canyon Trail. You're likely to be rewarded by the sight of golden eagles and other raptors. Several rock climbing routes along this trail are closed during the spring and summer in order to prevent disturbance of nest sites in the cliffs around Sheep Mountain.

The BALD EAGLE
Majestic Migrator

Bald eagles *(Haliaeetus leucocephalus)* are considered by many to be indicators of a clean and healthy environment. Ironically, however, visitors will find few of America's national symbols within Rocky Mountain National Park. These distinctive raptors appear almost exclusively as migratory flyers passing near the park every autumn on their way from Canada to winter feeding areas in southern Colorado.

Although there are no active bald eagle nesting sites in the park, the birds attract attention when they are spotted by virtue of their size and instant recognizability. They are listed as an endangered species in 43 states and are protected by the International Migratory Bird Treaty.

Bald eagles have been uniquely imprinted upon the American psyche for more than two centuries. In 1782 Congress selected the bald eagle as the national symbol of the United States—over the objections of Benjamin Franklin, who wanted instead to honor the wild turkey. Franklin argued that the eagle's reputation and lifestyle was not noble enough, but few today would maintain that Congress made the wrong choice. When perched in a tree, a majestic, full-grown bald eagle stands between 2-1/2 and 3 feet tall; when cruising over a waterway, its extended wings span six to seven feet.

As everyone familiar with the species knows, bald eagles are not truly bald. Their name is derived from the Greek word *leucocephalus*, meaning "white-headed." The bird's crown and tail feathers take on their famed snow-white hue only when it reaches adulthood. The process of maturation may take four to five years and involves five distinct molts (feather sheddings). In the meantime, observers unfamiliar with the brown phase markings of immature bald eagles often confuse them with golden eagles, which are more common in the park.

As Ben Franklin noted, bald eagles are not particularly picky in matters of diet. They hunt for live fish and scavenge for dead trout that wash up on the shore of a lake. Rocky Mountain does not contain a local population of bald eagles, because there are no lakes within park boundaries large enough to offer the birds a regular supply of fish and sufficient space to insulate them from intruders. But don't let that stop you from continuing your wildlife safari after you leave the park in spring and autumn. Over nearby lakes in the early morning hours, you may suddenly behold a bald eagle in your camera's viewfinder.

Where to Find Bald Eagles —
▶ Look for these raptors in late autumn on the bigger lakes outside the park, including Grand Lake, Shadow Mountain Lake, and Lake Grandby. Lake Estes is also used by bald eagles as a point of stopover.

The RED-TAILED HAWK
Rufous Raptor

The red-tailed hawk is by far the most common raptor in Rocky Mountain National Park; this is the bird of prey that visitors are most likely to spot gliding across the skies. In general, redtails *(Buteo jamaicensis)* are less wary of humans than golden eagles, peregrine falcons, and other birds of prey. The hawks hunt for rodents and small birds in open meadows and at the edges of forests in all elevations. Active throughout the day, they often provide wildlife watchers with an intimate look at the predator-prey relationship.

The redtail's wingspan measures four feet or more, and its markings are hard to miss. The adult bird is adorned with brownish feathers on top and a reddish (rufous) tail with a brown stripe that runs parallel to the bird's body. From the ground as the bird flies overhead, notice the redtail's lighter, rust-colored tail; its off-white underbelly decorated with wavy bands of brown; and the brown patches on its head. The same brown is present laterally across the shoulders and again on the wingtips. If this hawk isn't soaring above a meadow, you'll see it perched in a tree, watching for movement in the grass with its razor-sharp eyesight.

Where to Find Red-Tailed Hawks —
▶ Year-round residents of Rocky Mountain, redtails often move to lower elevations during the winter. During all other seasons, they are spotted from turnouts along Trail Ridge Road.
▶ Experienced birders may want to consider a hike from Twin Owls Trailhead north of Estes Park, a trek that offers premier raptor viewing in the cliffs and meadows along the Black Canyon Trail. Red-tailed hawks and several other birds of prey are routinely visible here. Remember that it is against park regulations to approach a nest. Several hiking and rock climbing routes in the northeast corner of the park are closed to accommodate birds during the nesting season.

The PEREGRINE FALCON
Bird on the Rebound

 Although the peregrine falcon is among the rarest of hawks, and is a species afforded protection on the federal list of endangered species, its return from near extinction is considered one of the great conservation success stories of the 20th century.

The peregrine *(Falco peregrinus)* was once widely distributed across North America, including Rocky Mountain National Park, but spraying of the pesticide DDT during the 1950s and 1960s sent these great raptors into a tailspin. According to federal wildlife officials, the peregrine was close to extinction east of the Mississippi River by 1960; ten years later, the same fate seemed to await falcons along the Rockies.

Fortunately, peregrines have begun to recover since DDT use was permanently banned in the early 1970s. Today, the National Park Service has joined forces with a conservation group called the Peregrine Fund in reintroducing the majestic bird to such parks as Rocky Mountain, Yellowstone, and Glacier.

A male peregrine can be identified by its intense features: dark gray head feathers that resemble a helmet with sideburns; pointed "falcon" wings and tail; and occasional dark streaks on its white chest. Females are a darker brown on top and bottom. Both males and females are about the size of ravens.

The peregrine's beauty is most apparent in flight. It moves at awesome speeds, and its acute eyesight makes it a very effective hunter of waterfowl and other birds. In urban areas, wildlife watchers have been surprised at the sight of reintroduced peregrines gliding between skyscrapers, in pursuit of pigeons. But the human imagination is most stimulated when peregrines are seen in their historic habitat.

According to ornithologists, the remote rock outcroppings of Rocky Mountain are excellent resting places for peregrines. It is vitally important that humans leave these birds of prey alone, particularly during the nesting season. Park officials are generally discreet about the exact locations of peregrine nests, or eyries. To minimize the disruption of peregrine nesting and foraging areas, Rocky Mountain closes several hiking and rock-climbing routes during the early summer, when the eggs are about to hatch.

Where to Find Peregrine Falcons —
▶ One of the best ways to view peregrines and other birds of prey entails a hike into the Lumpy Range from Twin Owls Trailhead north of Estes Park. Before you set out, check with park rangers to determine whether any of the trails or climbing routes are

closed to the public. Despite the peregrine's rarity in the park, roadside wildlife watchers occasionally see these birds gliding over meadows along Trail Ridge Road.

The CLARK'S NUTCRACKER
Pine Planter

The domain of the Clark's nutcracker *(Nucifraga columbiana)* is found in high ridge-lines, where incessant wind and brutal cold have contorted the trunks of ancient pines, spruce, and fir, and stunted the growth of juniper. It is an unforgiving environment, but one that seems warmer due to the presence of nutcrackers. They are big birds that reside in the park year-round, and their markings are obvious—a gray body accented by black on the wings and tail, with a splash of white on the wingtips and the outer tail feathers. The head is set off by black eyes and a long, pointed, dark-gray bill.

Clark's nutcrackers take their name from Capt. William Clark

71

of the Lewis and Clark Expedition, which charted a route from St. Louis to the Pacific Ocean between 1804 and 1806. Related to the crow, nutcrackers emit a *kraa* instead of a *kaw*, and they are so accustomed to people that they will try to steal food from campsites. Resist the temptation to feed them, for habituation to human handouts jeopardizes their survival over the long term. Instead, let them make their living on the available natural staples of seeds, animal carcasses, and berries.

In their quest to harvest seeds, Clark's nutcrackers throughout the Rockies have inadvertently become silviculturists, or cultivators of forest trees. After extracting conifer nuts from the cone, they bury the nuts in the ground for later consumption. But they fail to retrieve all of the seeds and, as a result, new seedlings sprout. Many trees in Rocky Mountain National Park owe their very existence to these high-altitude birds.

Where to Find Clark's Nutcrackers —
▶ The birds are abundant along Trail Ridge Road at altitudes above 10,000 feet, particularly along turnouts such as Farview Curve, Rainbow Curve, and Medicine Bow Curve. Visitors also encounter them along the paved road to Endovalley and the unpaved Fall River Road, which stretches farther to the Alpine Visitor Center.

The STELLER'S JAY
Crested Cousin

Imagine a blue jay flaunting a dark mohawk haircut. This is how one ornithologist described the Steller's jay *(Cyanocitta stelleri)*, an avian fixture in the coniferous forests of Rocky Mountain National Park. Besides boasting luminous blue plumage and an unforgettable gray head crest, Steller's jays are the only crested jay in the Rockies.

The head of a Steller's jay (known in some circles as the mountain jay) tends to be sooty black, while the belly, back, and wings are a deep, memorable blue. These cousins of the Eastern blue jay are frequent scavengers at campsites and turnouts, partly because past visitors have broken park regulations by feeding them.

Although Steller's jays are confined within the continental U.S. to areas west of the Rockies, they are found from Alaska to Central America. They often set up their nests in fir trees. Omnivores, they are like all members of the crow family in that they search aggressively for food. They eat insects, berries, seeds, and young birds. They frequently announce their presence in treetops, perching there as they look for their next meal, and they sometimes mimic the calls of other birds in order to frighten off competitors. It's a treat to observe Steller's jays, and they are ubiquitous within the park.

Where to Find Steller's Jays —
▶ Year-round residents, Steller's jays are often seen along Trail Ridge Road at Rainbow Curve, Forest Canyon Overlook, Rock Cut, and Medicine Bow Curve.

The MOUNTAIN BLUEBIRD
Turquoise Thrush

Amidst the brilliant shades of wildflowers that erupt on the alpine tundra every summer, mountain bluebirds *(Sialia currucoides)* add welcome flashes of turquoise. These alpine thrushes are typically spotted within the park at or slightly above the coniferous treeline.

Mountain bluebirds are summer residents in Rocky Mountain National Park, spending their winters in the southern U.S. and Mexico. Early-morning risers will hear their warbling notes as they move between trees and bushes or boulders in search of insects. Only males are blue on top, with a faint blue breast. Females are grayish-brown with touches of blue on their wings and tails.

The mountain bluebird's range overlaps somewhat with that of the Western bluebird, but they can generally be distinguished through differences in coloration among the male birds. There is an obvious streak of orange on the shoulders and breasts of Western bluebird males; the breasts of mountain bluebird males are entirely blue.

Mountain bluebirds nest at lower elevations, usually in aspen or conifer tree cavities created by woodpeckers. Near many mountain communities in Colorado, people have built special nesting boxes for bluebirds, but in the park the birds rely on what nature has provided. Bluebirds feed primarily on insects. They prepare to head south in early to mid autumn, after the first frosts have begun to extingush the birds' food supply.

Where to Find Mountain Bluebirds —
▶ Venture out after sunrise to find mountain bluebirds at the alluvial fan between Sheep Lakes and Endovalley; along Bear Lake Road; and at turnouts along Trail Ridge Road.

The BROAD-TAILED HUMMINGBIRD
Busy Buzzer

 In many campgrounds during the summer months, visitors hear a repeated buzzing that sounds like giant bumblebees. Don't let it fool you. The whirring emanates from the sputtering wings of broad-tailed hummingbirds *(Selasphorus platycercus)* that are busily searching for sweet nectar. It's inspiring to imagine this four-inch bird faithfully migrating between Rocky Mountain National Park and Central American jungles each year. In a small package, broadtails offer much insight about neo-tropical birds.

Their distinctive, neon-like markings include the male's rose-colored gorget (throat), white belly, and luminous, lime-green feathers on both the head and back. The female also has green on its back and tail, but the belly is pale brown and the head is somewhat darker. As the bird's name implies, its tail is wide and rounded like a fan.

The broad-tailed practices "philopatry," meaning it returns to the vicinity of its former nest year after after year. If the old nest has fallen apart or filled with parasites, as is often the case, the bird builds a new one near the old foundation.

Artificial feeding of hummingbirds is prohibited within Rocky Mountain National Park. Broadtails are one of 15 hummingbird species that breed in North America. Most make their home in montane meadows on the edge of a forest.

Where to Find Broad-Tailed Hummingbirds —
▶ Listen for them at the Timber Creek Campground in the
Kawuneeche Valley; at Aspenglen Campground near the Fall
River Entrance Station; and at Sandbeach Lake Trailhead along
Highway 7.

The WESTERN TANAGER
Tropical Traveler

When birders explore the subalpine forests
of Rocky Mountain National Park and spot a
western tanager, they gain a sensuous taste of
the tropics. The blazing red heads, equally
vivid yellow bodies, and black wings make the
male tanager an unforgettable sight. By contrast, females have green-
ish-yellow heads, kerchiefs of gray, and black wings. The wings of
both genders sport stripes of white and yellow.

Western tanagers *(Piranga ludoviciana)* commute seasonally between their summer breeding areas in North America and southern foraging ranges located as far south as Costa Rica. They are avian links between the rainforest and the stands of old-growth Douglas-fir and spruce that serve as their nesting areas. The songs of these birds are as striking as their appearance.

About 240 species of tanagers are found throughout much of the western hemisphere. However, the western tanager is one of only four species native to the U.S. and Canada. Perhaps the defining characteristics of most tanagers are their brilliant plumage and the similarities in their diet. They rely upon insects early in the summer, then switch to berries as the fruits ripen. Tanager nests are usually made of twigs and built high in pine trees. The female lays between one and five eggs.

Where to Find Western Tanagers —
▶ Look for western tanagers in the forest at Sprague Lake Campground along Bear Lake Road; west of Moraine Park near the Cub Lake Trailhead; and a little further south at Hollowell Park.

The WHITE-TAILED PTARMIGAN
Tundra Trotter

Visitors to the alpine tundra may notice a large ground bird whose feathers change with the seasons, blending with the environment. White-tailed ptarmigans *(Lagopus leucurus)* are avian chameleons. Their feathers are snowy white throughout the winter; then, following a spring molting, their plumage becomes a mottled brown that reflects the rocky terrain of summer.

Scientists say that ptarmigans (pronounced TAR-MUH-GUNS) thrive where alpine plant communities exist in a tundra environment. Such tundra, in the lower 48 states at least, is found only at northern latitudes and in isolated, high-elevation areas within the Rocky Mountain, Cascade, and Sierra-Nevada ranges.

The white-tailed ptarmigan is the smallest ptarmigan species and is related to the rock and willow ptarmigan, which are found in Canada and Alaska. Despite their soft, delicate appearance, white-tailed ptarmigans are hardy birds; they need to be in order to survive year-round in the wind- and snow-dominated environment of Rocky Mountain's alpine tundra. On the coldest days of winter, ptarmigans burrow into the snowpack, a tactic that insulates them from the bitter elements.

In summer, wildlife watchers scanning the alpine tundra off of Trail Ridge Road may have a difficult time spotting ptarmigans, for their camouflage helps them avoid coyotes, raptors, and foxes that prey upon them and their ground nests. The bird's summer phase finds it bedecked in brown-mottled feathers set off by white splashes on the tail, breast, and wings.

A member of a family of chicken-like birds and a close relative of many grouse species, the ptarmigan flies longer distances when flushed than its woodland grouse cousins, though it actually prefers to run when trying to evade intruders. Thick feathers on its feet enable the ptarmigan to trot across snow.

It is vitally important that wildlife watchers in the alpine tundra stay on established trails—not only to avoid disturbing ptarmigan, but to minimize physical impacts on the sensitive and often rare plant communities that thrive here.

Where to Find White-Tailed Ptarmigan —
▶ Look for ptarmigans from the Alpine Tundra Tail along Trail Ridge Road. Or take your time with binoculars or a spotting scope and try to locate them from the Old Fall River Road, which opens in early July. Ptarmigans forage for insects, leaves, and berries near rock outcroppings.

The WATER PIPIT
Arctic Avian

Water pipits (Anthus spinoletta) are marvelous creatures that occur primarily where high elevation and the accompanying plant communities create conditions similar to the tundra normally found in Alaska and northern Canada. The pipit is a ground dweller; it nests and forages in arctic-like conditions, nervously watching for predators or invaders of its stark terrain.

In appearance the water pipit, which is sometimes called the American pipit, resembles a brown sparrow. Notice the bird's brown cape, mottled-brown and off-white breast, and white chin and underbelly. Look also for the white feathers on the fringe of its tail. While its physical features are not extraordinary, the bird's adaptation to the highest terrestrial realm of the park is remarkable. It often shares its habitat with ptarmigans.

The pipit frequently puddle-hops, ingesting insects that collect in the water after they're carried upward by winds from the valleys below. Pipits also search the snowpack, and in early summer they reach the most remote meadows off Trail Ridge Road before the highway is even open to tourist traffic.

Water pipits are one of five pipit species in North America. The bird summers in Rocky Mountain, but it spends the harshest winter months as far south as Guatemala. Listen for the call of the pipit overhead—it issues a sonorous *jee-itt* that can sound a bit like its name.

Where to Find Water Pipits —
▶ Walk the Alpine Tundra Trail from Rock Cut off Trail Ridge Road. Or scout for pipits from Old Fall River Road, which is gravel and remains closed until the first part of July. You can also try to spot these birds as they search for insects on top of snowfields.

A ROCKY MOUNTAIN GALLERY

Greenback Cutthroat Trout
Salmo clarki stomias

While there are plenty of furry and feathered creatures to watch in the park, one of the rarest species here happens to be a fish. The greenback cutthroat trout is protected as "threatened" under the federal Endangered Species Act, because it has disappeared from most of its former range. At one time, this native subspecies was found in headwaters of the South Platte and Arkansas rivers, but today's recovery effort centers on a few places within Rocky Mountain National Park. In fact, a special trout viewing area has been designed at Hidden Valley Beaver Ponds along Trail Ridge Road, offering visitors a novel opportunity to see the trout up-close in its original habitat. The greenback can be identified by its conspicuous reddish color, and by black spots that are large and concentrated toward the tail. Spawning takes place in spring and early summer.

Pine Marten
Martes americana

Like all members of the weasel family, pine martens are aggressive for their size. Although these tree-dwelling carnivores are elusive in the presence of humans, they kill red squirrels or chipmunks, and

they raid bird nests fearlessly. The animal owes part of its agility to its strong, short legs, and to claws that enable it to climb with ease. Fur trappers once dubbed the marten "American sable" because of the luxurious feel and warmth of its fur. Active year-round, the pine marten resembles a brown-phase weasel, but it is a larger animal with a tail one-third as long as its tubular body. Watch for pine martens throughout park woodlands, but especially in the vicinity of Bear Lake Trailhead, the Never Summer Ranch, and the Timber Creek Campground.

Long-Tailed Weasel
Mustela frenata

Neurotic, curious, and highly predatory, weasels move so subtly through the landscape that they often go unnoticed. But if you are patient and peer silently through a spotting scope or binoculars, you may see one of the park's most efficient hunters at work. Within Rocky Mountain, there is no carnivore with a greater distribution than the long-tailed weasel. A long-tail's coat is brown with a light tan underside during the summer; it changes to white in winter, reflecting the snowy surroundings. At maturity, an adult weighs less than eight ounces, yet it takes on prey twice its size. Long-tails are found at all elevations—in meadows and woodlands, near campgrounds, and in the remotest wilderness outpost. Visitors may also spot short-tailed weasels *(Mustela erminea)*, which are known to some people as ermine and weigh even less than long-tails. Both species are abundant and prey upon mice, voles, chipmunks, and birds.

Raccoon
Procyon lotor

The higher elevations of Rocky Mountain are beyond the normal limits of the raccoon's range, but these well-known nocturnal scavengers are found in abundance along the park's eastern border. Campers in Estes Park should take every possible measure to secure food inside their car, lest it fall victim to raiding raccoons. Although these animals appear tame, they are not, and visitors are reminded that feeding wildlife is against park regulations. Raccoons are found across the United States and are native only to the Americas. They are readily identifiable by the black "mask" markings on their faces, their gray bodies, and their bushy, dark-ringed tails. Raccoons are omnivores that weigh between 20 and 45 pounds, depending on the local natural food supply and whether humans have been feeding them. Breeding takes place during the winter, and a litter of about four or five young is born in April or May. Look for raccoons "fishing" along streams in lower elevations.

Muskrat
Ondatra zibethicus

Muskrats inhabit many of Rocky Mountain's waterways, but the best muskrat habitat in the park is found west of the Continental Divide. In a shallow pond setting, the muskrat's house— constructed of cattails, reeds, mud, and twigs— resembles a miniature beaver lodge. Indeed, these aquatic rodents live in the wetland environment created by beavers. In lakes or streams that are not conducive to  lodges, the brown-furred muskrat builds a den in the bank or shoreline and accesses it through a tunnel in the water called a "run." A muskrat's tail is long, flattened, and leathery. Its hind feet are webbed, but the front paws are clawed, allowing it to grasp the plants, crawfish, and fish that make up its diet. Muskrats remain active in winter. Look for them in the early morning and evening hours along the Colorado River.

Striped Skunk
Mephitis mephitis

Chances are, you will smell a skunk in the park long before you see one; you'll almost certainly notice the odor at lower elevations, probably near the three major entrance stations. The striped skunk is seen sparingly around developments inside the park, but it's more common in developed areas along the park's perimeter.

As its name implies, the striped skunk sports two white stripes on its black body. It is most active at night, and you are well advised to keep a clean camp in order to prevent a skunk invasion. The infrequently observed cousin of the striped skunk is the Western spotted skunk (*Spilogale gracilis*). It has irregular stripes that look like spots on its back. Both species are capable of defending themselves by secreting the skunk's trademark, powerful spray, which originates in glands near the animal's posterior. They do so

whenever threatened by intruders, including people and domestic pets. The presence of skunks offers another compelling reason why pet owners should keep their animals restrained at all times.

Nuttall's Cottontail
Sylvilagus nuttalli

The Nuttall's cottontail is the smaller and more colorful cousin of the snowshoe hare. It has a classic rabbit body, a gray coat that in summer may change to brown, and black-tipped ears. It lives on the edge of the coniferous forest, often among sagebrush and upland grasslands, but it has been seen throughout the park. The Nuttall's feet and ears are shorter than those of a snowshoe hare. Like snowshoes, the Nuttall's is preyed upon by bobcats, coyotes, foxes, hawks, and owls. Look for Nuttall's cottontails along the Bear Lake Road and near the Fall River Entrance Station around dusk and dawn.

Golden-Mantled Squirrel
Spermophilus lateralis

The golden-mantled ground squirrel is often mistaken for a chipmunk. Golden-mantles are found in most coniferous forests as you approach treeline. They play an important role in the park's food chain, for they are

preyed upon by badgers, coyotes, foxes, many different raptors, and small predators including weasels. Like chipmunks, golden-mantles have readily recognized white and black stripes across their gray backs. They share an affinity with marmots—each rodent species hibernates in its underground den from early autumn until spring. Vegetarians, golden-mantled squirrels eat grasses, insects, berries, and nuts, and are often seen collecting food in their cheek pouches. Look for them at Rainbow Curve and other turnouts along Trail Ridge Road. Another notable squirrel, the Wyoming ground squirrel *(Spermophilus elegans)* bears a strong resemblance to gophers, and can often be seen from Trail Ridge Road near Farview Curve. Generally, Wyoming ground squirrels inhabit open sagebrush meadows and parks. They often stand on their hind feet, surveying the landscape for food and watching for predators.

Red Squirrel (Chickaree)
Tamiasciurus hudsonicus

Whether known as chickarees, red squirrels, or pine squirrels, one thing is certain about the orange-gray rodents that nest in trees: They are abundant in Rocky Mountain National Park. Red squirrels are the smallest squirrel species in the park, weighing between five and eight ounces. They inhabit ponderosa pine and subalpine forests, and they're visible around most hiking trails and campgrounds at lower elevations. During the spring and summer, red squirrels build nests out of twigs and mosses; in the harsh winter months, they relocate to tree holes that offer protection from the cold. They are productive gatherers of fruits, vegetables, and nuts, and their primary enemies include pine martens, bobcats, and birds of prey, especially owls.

American Dipper
Cinclus mexicanus

The dipper makes its home along most of the park's faster-moving streams. Slate-gray, it has the frame of a wren and the zeal of water-fowl; in fact, it's called "water ouzel" by some people. A permanent resident of Rocky Mountain, the stubby-tailed

dipper is found from Alaska to Panama; it forages and nests on the edge of rapids, where it finds an abundance of insects. Amazingly, these small aquatic songbirds appear to skim across the surface of rivers, and they are occasionally seen diving into the chilly flows and running along the bottom of a stream—sometimes with their wings extended. Their feathers, however, do not get soaked. Oil is naturally secreted by their bodily glands (much like the oil that protects diving ducks), so their plumage actually repels water. Typically, a dipper will construct its spherical, mossy nest so that it faces the stream. Look for dippers in streams along Bear Lake Road, along the Fall River, and along the Big Thompson River east of Estes Park. You may even spot them during the harshest winter months in areas where the water stays open and free of ice.

Common Snipe
Gallinago gallinago

Common snipe are almost mythical birds. Some people refuse to believe that the birds really exist. In Rocky Mountain, however, they are found virtually everywhere. The moist, willow-lined riverbottoms provide nesting and foraging cover, and snipe are never far from water. The common snipe is recognized for its long, thin bill and its mottled-brown feather pattern. Flushing a hidden snipe, hearing it cluck, and watching it rocket across a meadow is a memorable experience. During the breeding season male snipe, like male grouse, perform a feather-drumming ritual. However, the snipe's ritual is performed in mid-flight. The male flies in a circular pattern, then descends, creating a dull noise that attracts female snipe by flexing his tail feathers. The birds are primarily summer residents of the park.

Raven
Corvus corvax

Although several members of the crow family are represented within the park, the raven has all of the classic crow markings and is the largest such bird seen here. Big, black, and larger than a crow, the raven is found near most of the campgrounds and scenic turnouts along the roadside. Talkative and unafraid of people, it will often announce its presence with a bois-terous kraaaak-krah that is distinct from the crow's kaw. The raven can also be distinguished from the crow by the scruffy feathers around its throat and head and its longer beak, which often has feathers on top. Ravens may be seen soaring like raptors, whereas crows tend to flap their wings in flight. Ravens may bully songbirds by raiding their nests and eating young birds or consuming eggs; on the other hand, they do not hesitate to nourish themselves on carrion.

Black-Billed Magpie
Pica pica

Black-billed magpies are common along many stretches of park highway that pass through open shrub meadows and mixed forest. The magpies are large, enterprising scavengers known for raiding trash cans in developed areas. In Rocky Mountain, magpies find sustenance in winter-kill carcasses, grasshoppers, moths, and other insects. Visitors should be mindful of the fact that feeding wildlife in the park is punishable by a fine.

Few wildlife watchers ever forget the decorative markings of a black-billed magpie. The black-bill's scientific name means black and white, and it describes the bird perfectly. It has penetrating black plumage that covers the head and runs the length of the back across a long tail. Part of its underside and front scapular, however, is bright white. When the bird flies, the white patches flap back and forth. The bird has a black bill. Magpies are year-round residents of the park. Look for them on the edge of ponderosa pine forests. They are regular visitors to the Sheep Lakes area of Horseshoe Park, the Many Parks Curve on Trail Ridge Road, and the Bear Lake Road.

Gray Jay
Perisoreus canadensis

The gray jay comes from the same family of birds as Clark's nutcrackers, black-billed magpies, and Steller's jays. All are members of the crow tribe, and all are common in Rocky Mountain. Wildlife watchers will typically see gray jays year-round, perched in conifers along the roadside looking for something to eat. Gray jays are solid light gray across the back and tail, but their plumage is highlighted by white undersides and black "caps" on their heads. Their bills are less conspicuous than those of the other members of the crow family. Refrain from feeding these birds; instead, take delight in watching them forage for natural foods. Look for gray jays at Many Parks, Rainbow Curve, and along Bear Lake Road.

Mallard
Anas platyrhynchos

Abundant across most of the United States, found in city parks and wilderness wetlands, the mallard is by far the most universally recognized

duck. These waterfowl nest and reside year-round in Rocky Mountain and are found on both sides of the Continental Divide. Drakes are unmistakable. They have yellow bills, green heads, darkish feathers about the neck, chestnut breasts, and white bellies. Hens are mottled brown in color, distinguished by a yellowish bill, orange, webbed feet, and a pattern of white, black, and purple on their wings. Mother mallards issue the classic duck call, *quack wak wak*, when they're looking after young ducklings or calling to other ducks on the pond.

Blue Grouse
Dendragapus obscurus

A resident of brushy ridgelines, the blue grouse is occasionally spotted along the roadside, but it more often surprises backcountry hikers who inadvertently startle it. This large game bird, which is hunted outside the park, is granted refuge within Rocky Mountain, so it may become accustomed to human presence. The blue grouse is a non-migratory relative of

the white-tailed ptarmigan. It forages on grasshoppers, juniper berries, and other plants during the warm seasons, but switches to conifer needles as a winter staple. Contrary to its name, the male grouse is not truly blue, but a faint, bluish gray; the male flaunts an orange-gray comb near its eyes and a purple pouch that becomes visible during the spring mating dance. Hens are brown. The courtship jig is conducted by the male, which tries to gain the attention of hens by filling and deflating its neck pouch, emitting what some ornithologists calls "booms" and "hoots." The dance is often performed on a log. The blue grouse moves to higher elevations in winter, burrowing into the snowpack as insulation against the cold. Look for blue grouse in the subalpine forest along Trail Ridge Road, the Old Fall River Trail, and the Bear Lake Road.

SO YOU'D LIKE TO KNOW MORE?

Here is a list of sources that offer more information about wildlife watching opportunities in Rocky Mountain National Park:

NATIONAL PARK SERVICE: Park rangers are happy to tell you when the elk start bugling, when the shuttle bus to Bear Lake is running, when the bighorn sheep can be seen near Horseshoe Park, and when Trail Ridge Road has opened for the summer. In addition, the Park Service offers a free brochure entitled "Ski Touring in Rocky Mountain National Park," which suggests several routes for cross country skiers. If you have questions previous to your visit, call Rocky Mountain National Park at (303) 586-2371.

ROCKY MOUNTAIN NATURE ASSOCIATION: This non-profit organization has done a terrific job of educating the public about the plants and animals found in Rocky Mountain National Park. By supporting the Association, you help protect flora and fauna, and you ensure that wildlife watching opportunities will exist for future park visitors. The Association sponsors nature walks, presents slide shows and lectures about the ecosystem, and publishes books about the park's natural history. For membership information, write to: Rocky Mountain Nature Association, Rocky Mountain National Park, Estes Park, CO 80517.

CAMPING
Reservations are required for campsites at Moraine Park and Glacier Basin campgrounds. All other roadside campsites are available on a first-come, first-served basis. Backcountry permits are required for wilderness campsites. There are about 355 miles of hiking trails within the park. For campsite information, call the Park Service's backcountry camping office at (303) 586-4459.

ACCOMMODATIONS
There are no motels or hotels within the park. For information about overnight accommodations near the park, or to hire natural history guides, contact the chamber of commerce in Estes Park, CO 80517, or Grand Lake, CO 80447.

FURTHER READING

Wildlife watchers who would enjoy a thorough account of mammalian natural history in Rocky Mountain will find just such an account in David M. Armstrong's book, *Rocky Mountain Mammals*. The book provides an in-depth narrative concerning 66 species of mammals, and it is available at all park visitor centers. The volume is published in cooperation with the Rocky Mountain Nature Association.

BIBLIOGRAPHY

Allen, Thomas B. eds. Wild Animals of North America.
National Geographic Society, 1979.

Alden, Peter. Peterson First Guides, Mammals.
Houghton Mifflin Co., 1987.

Armstrong, David M. Rocky Mountain Mammals.
Colorado Associated University Press, 1987.

"Beware Bears!" National Park Service pamphlet.
U.S. Government Printing Office, 1993.

Books, Dave. "Identification of Montana's Upland Game Birds."
Distributed by Montana Department of Fish, Wildlife, and Parks;
reprinted by Montana Outdoors Magazine.

Brainerd, Scott. "Those Small Montana Wild Cats."
Montana Outdoors Magazine, November/December 1989.

Caldwell, Douglas, Rocky Mountain National Park's public affairs officer.
Personal communication, 1993.

"Call of the Wapiti." National Park Service pamphlet.
U.S. Government Printing Office, 1992.

Clark, W.S. and M.E. Pramstaller. Field I.D.Guide for North American
Raptors. Raptor Information Center,
National Wildlife Federation, Washington D.C., 1980.

Crabtree, Dr. Robert. Numerous communications between 1987 and 1993.

Craighead, J.J. and F.C. Craighead, Jr. Hawks, Owls and Wildlife.
Dover Publications, 1969.

Halfpenny, James. A Field Guide to Mammal Tracking in Western America.
Johnson Books, 1986.

Herrero, Stephen. Bear Attacks: Their Causes and Avoidance.
Nick Lyons Books, 1985.

High Country Headlines, Rocky Mountain National Park newspaper,
1992 and 1993 summer issues.

Holt, Harold R. & James A. Lane. A Birder's Guide to Colorado.
ABA Sales, 1988.

Matthiessen, Peter. Wildlife in America. Viking Penguin, 1987.

Mays, Buddy. Guide to Western Wildlife. Chronicle Books, 1977.

Maugans, Jeff. Personal communication, 1993.

Melbo, Irving R. Our Country's National Parks, Volume Two.
The Bobbs-Merrill Company, 1941.

Miller Jr., Arthur P. *Park Ranger Guide to Wildlife.* Stackpole Books, 1990.

Miller, Millie, and Cyndi Nelson. *Talons: North American Birds of Prey.* Johnson Books, 1989.

Mills, Enos A. *Wild Life on the Rockies.* University of Nebraska Press, 1988.

Murie, Adolph. "Ecology of the Coyote in the Yellowstone." U.S. Government Printing Office, 1940.

Murie, Olaus J. *Animal Tracks.* Houghton Mifflin Company, 1974.

Murie, Olaus J. *The Elk of North America.* Stackpole Company, 1951.

"National Park Service Management Policies." Prepared by U.S. Department of the Interior.

National Parks of the West. Lane Magazine & Book Company, 1965.

Parker, Steve. *Mammal: Eyewitness Books.* Alfred A. Knopf, 1989.

Peregrine Fund, Inc. Operation reports published at the World Center for Birds of Prey, 1990-1991.

Peterson, David. *Racks: The Natural History of Antlers and the Animals That Wear Them.* Capra Press, 1991.

Peterson, Roger Tory. *Western Birds.* Houghton Mifflin Company, 1990.

Reel, Susan, Lisa Schassberger, and William Ruediger. "Caring for our Natural Community: Threatened, Endangered and Sensitive Species Program, Northern Region of U.S. Forest Service." 1989.

Richie, Deborah. "Underwater Flier." *Montana Outdoors Magazine,* July/August 1992

"Rocky Mountain Bighorn." National Park Service pamphlet.

"Rocky Mountain: A Student's Guide to Park Resources." National Park Service pamphlet. U.S. Government Printing Office, 1992.

"Rocky Mountain National Park Final Land Protection Plan." U.S. Department of the Interior, 1984

Russo, Ron. *Mountain State Mammals.* Illustrated by Barbara Downs. Nature Study Guild, 1991.

Schmidt, John L., and Douglas L. Gilbert. *Big Game of North America.* Stackpole Books, 1978.

"Science and the National Parks." Report on science in national parks prepared by National Research Council. National Academy Press, 1992.

Stall, Chris. *Animal Tracks of the Rocky Mountains.* The Mountaineers, 1989.

Stelfox, Brad. "Wildlife Info Cards." Prepared for Teton Science School.

Wildlife of the American West Museum: Jackson, WY.

Tilden, Freeman. *The National Parks.* Alfred A. Knopf, 1968.

Udvardy, Miklos D.F. *The Audubon Society Field Guide to North American Mammals.* Alfred A. Knopf, 1977.

Ulrich, Tom J. *Mammals of the Northern Rockies.* Mountain Press Publishing, 1986.

Watchable Wildlife. Publication of the Bureau of Land Management in conjunction with Defenders of Wildlife, 1990.

Whitaker Jr. John O., *The Audubon Society Field Guide to North American Mammals.* Alfred A. Knopf, 1980.

Whitney, Stephen. *Western Forests.* Alfred A. Knopf, Third Printing, 1988.

Wilkinson, Todd. *Glacier Park Wildlife: A Watcher's Guide.* NorthWord Press, 1993.

Wilkinson, Todd. *Yellowstone Wildlife: A Watcher's Guide.* NorthWord Press, 1992.

Willard, Beatrice E. & Ann E. Zwinger. *Land Above the Trees: A Guide to the American Alpine.* Harper and Row Publishers, 1972.

Other Books in NorthWord's National Park Wildlife Watcher's Series:

Yellowstone Wildlife: A Watcher's Guide

Glacier Park Wildlife: A Watcher's Guide to Glacier Park and Waterton Lakes Park